A History of the LMS:
The Record-Breaking 'Thirties, 1931–39

'Steam Past' Books from Allen & Unwin

THE LIMITED by O. S. Nock
THE BIRTH OF BRITISH RAIL by Michael R. Bonavia
STEAM'S INDIAN SUMMER by George Heiron and Eric Treacy
GRAVEYARD OF STEAM by Brian Handley
PRESERVED STEAM IN BRITAIN by Patrick B. Whitehouse
MEN OF THE GREAT WESTERN by Peter Grafton
TRAVELLING BY TRAIN IN THE EDWARDIAN AGE by Philip Unwin
MAUNSELL'S NELSONS by D. W. Winkworth
MAN OF THE SOUTHERN: JIM EVANS LOOKS BACK by Jim Evans
TRAINS TO NOWHERE: BRITISH STEAM TRAIN ACCIDENTS 1906–1960 by J. A. B. Hamilton
TRAVELLING BY TRAIN IN THE 'TWENTIES AND 'THIRTIES by Philip Unwin
MEN OF THE LNER by Peter Grafton
ON AND OFF THE RAILS by Sir John Elliot
THE RIDDLES STANDARD TYPES IN TRAFFIC by G. Freeman Allen
A HISTORY OF THE LNER by Michael R. Bonavia: I. The Early Years, 1923–33
A HISTORY OF THE LMS by O. S. Nock: I. The First Years, 1923–30
II. The Record-Breaking 'Thirties, 1931–39

STEAM, a year book edited by Roger Crombleholme and Terry Kirtland

A History of the LMS
II. The Record-Breaking 'Thirties, 1931–39

O. S. Nock B.Sc., C.Eng., F.I.C.E., F.I.Mech.E.

STEAM PAST

London
GEORGE ALLEN & UNWIN
Boston Sydney

George Allen & Unwin (Publishers) Ltd,
40 Museum Street, London WC1A 1LU, UK

George Allen & Unwin (Publishers) Ltd,
Park Lane, Hemel Hempstead, Herts HP2 4TE, UK

Allen & Unwin Inc.,
9 Winchester Terrace, Winchester, Mass 01890, USA

George Allen & Unwin Australia Pty Ltd,
8 Napier Street, North Sydney, NSW 2060, Australia

First published in 1982

British Library Cataloguing in Publication Data

Nock, O. S.
A history of the LMS.
Vol. 2: The record-breaking 'thirties, 1931–39
1. London, Midland and Scottish Railway – History
385'.0941 HE3020.L75
ISBN 0-04-385093-6

Set in 10 on 12 point Bembo by Nene Phototypesetters Ltd
and printed in Great Britain by
Biddles Ltd, Guildford, Surrey

Contents

Illustrations

Line drawings

I
Weathering the Slump

The year 1931 marked the climax of the crisis, economically and politically into which the country had been drifting for several years. There was general and severe depression in trade; shipbuilding and the heavy industries had very few orders, and this in turn greatly reduced the demand for coal. All this brought a great recession in railway freight traffic, which had of course been by far the greatest source of revenue, in past years, to railways like the London and North Western and the Midland, and to a lesser extent the Lancashire and Yorkshire and the Caledonian. The former Furness line was hit particularly hard. Furthermore, the depression was world-wide and certain European countries, and particularly the United States, were affected far more seriously than was Great Britain. It was against this sombre background that Sir Josiah Stamp continued his reconstruction of the top-level organisation. In no area was this more important than that of mechanical engineering in view of the high capital and maintenance costs involved.

The appointment of E. J. H. Lemon as Chief Mechanical Engineer, and the sideways move of Sir Henry Fowler to be assistant to Sir Harold Hartley, in January 1931, could soon after be seen as no more than interim measures, though the move of the Chief Mechanical Engineer's headquarters from Derby to Euston could be regarded as significant. At the same time recognition was at last given to the sterling work done at Crewe for so many years by H. P. M. Beames, by his appointment as Deputy Chief Mechanical Engineer. As Lemon was essentially a carriage and wagon man it seemed evident that Beames had been appointed to look after the locomotive side, although S. J. Symes, who had been personal assistant to Sir Henry Fowler, at Derby, was moved to Euston in a similar capacity to Lemon. But Stamp was looking further ahead. Follows was due to retire at the end of the year, and a Vice-President would be needed to take responsibility for the operating and commercial branches. Lemon, in fact, was booked for this job, and he was charged with the task of finding a new chief mechanical engineer. Although he had not many years to go Beames could well have looked forward, at last, to succeeding to the post that many felt should have been his by right from 1923, as one who had already held the eminent position of CME of the London and North Western Railway. But Stamp felt that the fires of old feuds would have been fanned again by the appointment of a man who still retained pronounced North Western sentiments, and the decision was taken to seek a complete outsider.

So, William Arthur Stanier, then Principal Assistant to the CME of the Great Western,

1. Sir Josiah Stamp, afterwards Baron Stamp of Shortlands: President of the Executive from 1926; Chairman from 1927.

Keystone

received an invitation to lunch from Lemon, to discuss some technical points about water softening. On the appointed day, however, Stanier was surprised to find Sir Harold Hartley also there. Certainly there was much talk about water softening, but Stanier was mystified. A short time afterwards he received another lunch invitation this time from Sir Harold himself, and in pleasant surroundings, at the Travellers Club, the suggestion of leaving the Great Western and joining the LMS as Chief Mechanical Engineer was put to him. Nigh twenty years ago when I was writing his biography Stanier told me how utterly surprised he was at the suggestion. Born and bred on the GWR, as it were, and completely happy in his work at Swindon he had not given the slightest thought to leaving. But the LMS offer, quite unofficial though it was at that stage, was so attractive as to put a different complexion on it. He told his chief, C. B. Collett, who in turn reported it to Sir James Milne. Thereafter it became official with Sir Josiah Stamp writing to Viscount Churchill, Chairman of the GWR; and so, on

New Year's Day 1932, with Follows retiring, Lemon moved up to Vice-President, and Stanier took office at Euston, as Chief Mechanical Engineer.

He took over the departmental organisation exactly as it had been under E. J. H. Lemon, though the first changes, which took place within a year, were caused by the retirement of J. E. Anderson from the office of Superintendent of Motive Power, which he had held since the formation of the LMS in 1923. To fill this vacancy David C. Urie was appointed. A son of R. W. Urie, the distinguished Chief Mechanical Engineer of the London and South Western Railway, he was the last locomotive superintendent of the Highland Railway, having succeeded Christopher Cumming in that office in April 1922. He had previously been assistant locomotive superintendent of the Midland Great Western Railway, in Ireland. Since the Grouping of the railways he had been divisional mechanical engineer in Glasgow, whereas his new appointment was on the operating side and thus independent of the CME; the position he had vacated in Scotland was not so, and to fill it H. G. Ivatt went, from his previous office of Works Superintendent, Derby. The Scottish appointment became regarded as a stepping stone to higher office, as will be clear from staff changes later in this particular period. So far as the operating side was concerned Urie remained in office as Superintendent of Motive Power until his retirement in 1943, a lengthy innings of more than ten years.

A small though important conversion to electric traction in the Manchester area was completed in May 1931. In pre-Grouping days the Manchester, South Junction and Altrincham line had been jointly owned by the Great Central and London and North Western Railways, and as such became a joint concern of the LNER and LMS. When the decision was taken to electrify

2. Sir Harold Hartley, Vice-President (Works and Ancillary Undertakings) and Director of Scientific Research, from 1930.

this very busy suburban line responsibility for all the work was vested in the LMS, which had in Lt-Col F. A. Cortez-Leigh, the Electrical Engineer, a senior officer of long and wide experience, having been responsible for the Euston electrification of the LNWR. The importance of the MSJ&A installation was that it was the first example in the country of the recommendations of the Weir Committee on main line electrification, set up by the Ministry of Transport in September 1929. In the report the 1,500-volt d.c. system was favoured with overhead current collection. This remained the recommended system even at the time when

C. R. L. Coles

3. A fine action shot of one of the Baby Scot class 5X 4–6–0s, no. 45551, on a down Blackpool express approaching Hatch End.

the British Railways Modernisation plan was launched, though this was subsequently changed in view of more recent experience elsewhere.

The Manchester, South Junction and Altrincham scheme involved the conversion to electric traction of the entire length of that railway between Manchester, London Road, and Altrincham, where an end-on junction was made with the Northwich line of the Cheshire Lines Committee. The only part of the MSJ&A not electrified was the short spur connecting with the main Liverpool and Manchester line of the LNWR near Ordsall Lane, a connection sometimes used when diversions are needed from the West Coast main line. As modernised, there were ten intermediate stations in the 8½ miles between London Road (now Piccadilly) and Altrincham, and stopping at all stations the journey time was twenty-four minutes. In a three-car multiple unit train there was seating for 228 third-class and forty first-class passengers. The composition of a standard train was third-class motor coach, composite first and third trailer, and third trailer, with driving compartment.

Another important suburban traffic development lay in the widening to quadruple track of the former London, Tilbury and Southend main line between Barking and Upminster, and the electrification of the new line, on the fourth rail system, to enable London Underground trains, hitherto terminating at Barking, to run through to Upminster if required. In this 7¾-mile section of quadruple track two new stations, Upney and Heathway, were built to be served only by the electrified tracks, while Becontree,

National Railway Museum

4. New electric stock on the Manchester South Junction and Altrincham line.

Dagenham, and Hornchurch were remodelled to serve four tracks. The electrified lines were equipped with automatic colour light signals, with electric train stops co-acting; and in connection with the latter a novel system of automatic control was installed. At that time, under automatic signalling rules trains that were pulled up at a stop signal were required to wait one minute, and then to proceed cautiously. Complete obedience to this rule was provided by means of a time-element relay which, on clearing after one minute, released the train stop and displayed a small yellow light beneath the main signal aspect, which remained at red. The release of the train stop and the clearing of the yellow light was, of course, contingent upon the overlap of the main signal being clear.

Another interesting case of track widening, but one involving much heavier civil engineering work was on the historic North Midland main line, built by George Stephenson and opened for traffic in 1840. This had already been

Author's Collection

5. A Royal Scot class 4–6–0 with the smoke deflectors fitted after the Leighton Buzzard accident: no. 6143, 'The South Staffordshire Regiment', originally named 'Mail'. The engine has the original narrow tender, but with coal rails added.

widened to quadruple track between Derby and Duffield, but had remained double-tracked to the Ambergate junctions. At that time there was heavy traffic on both the Manchester line, through the Peak District, and also on the North Midland line proper; and congestion occurred on the double-line length between Duffield and Ambergate. The widening works began in May 1930 and involved the provision of two new running lines for 1½ miles south of Ambergate to the crossing of the River Derwent at Broadholme Viaduct. Although there was no change at this latter point the widening of the line involved new viaducts at Dunge and in the approach to Ambergate where the railway again crossed the River Derwent. The new structures consisted of plate girders with rolled beams and concrete floors to carry the ballast on which ordinary sleepered track was laid. The viaducts were of no great height because the river was not navigable on this stretch, and at Ambergate the girders were supported on masonry piers.

Immediately to the south of the river crossing at Ambergate the line cuts through the Longland ridge where the rails are some 70 ft below ground level, and where George Stephenson carried the line in a short tunnel with a massive yet picturesque semi-circular arched portal at the Ambergate end. Although very heavy excavation would be involved it was decided to replace the tunnel by a deep cutting, much of it in solid rock. Because of the nature of the ground the cutting sides could be made very steep for about two thirds of the depth, having a slope of about $\frac{1}{4}$ to 1. At the top of the rock strata the ground was cut level for a short distance on each side and then tapered at $1\frac{1}{2}$ to 1, to the surface of the ground on either side of the railway. No less than 1,000,000 cubic yards of stone and shale needed to be removed. In the demolition of the tunnel the arch was bared and then broken down by blasting in sections of 45 ft long. Interesting though the engineering work was, however, one felt it was taking no more than half a bite at the traffic problem, while the double-line section between Broadholme Viaduct, through Belper, remained. It was fortunate, ultimately, that this latter widening was never carried out, for it included the Milford Tunnel with its stupendous semi-circular north facade. How the economically-minded George Stephenson came to include a work that is worthy of Brunel at his most flamboyantly grandiose baffles the imagination. It deserves to be scheduled as a historic building!

The Broadholme–Ambergate widening was one of the last works for which the Chief Engineer of the LMS, Alexander Newlands, was responsible; for he retired early in 1933. He was no stranger to rock excavation, for his first railway assignment, in 1893, had been to plan and carry out the westward extension of the Highland Railway from Strome Ferry to the Kyle of Lochalsh; and he was later involved in the widening of the main line between Blair Atholl and Dalwhinnie, which again involved some heavy rock cutting work. In 1914 he had been appointed Engineer-in-Chief of the Highland Railway, and as recorded in Volume One of the present work Chief Engineer of the LMS in 1927. His successor, W. K. Wallace, had, until September 1930, a career based entirely in Northern Ireland, on the Northern Counties Committee Section of the Midland Railway and later of the LMS. In 1922 he had succeeded Bowman Malcolm in the dual office of Locomotive Superintendent and Permanent Way Engineer, but in 1930 he crossed the water to become Chief Stores Superintendent of the LMS.

Reverting to the year 1931 reference must be made to the disastrous accident to the down Sunday 'Royal Scot' express at Leighton Buzzard, on 22 March. Because of engineering work farther north the train was to be diverted from the fast to the slow line at that station, a crossover movement that required a reduction of speed to 20 mph. For some reason, unexplained because of the deaths of the driver and fireman in the ensuing derailment, the train took the crossover road at about 55 mph; the engine overturned, the first three coaches were completely wrecked, and the fourth badly damaged. Fortunately, the train was not very full or the casualty list would have been much higher, with no more than six persons, including the driver and fireman, killed. While the Inspecting Officer of the Ministry of Transport, Lieut-Col A. H. L. Mount, could come to no definite conclusion as to why the driver should have ignored the warning of the distant signal 'on', and the home signal also kept at danger, suspicion

6. Mr (afterwards Sir William) Stanier, Chief Mechanical Engineer from January 1932.

Author's Collection

centred upon the possibility of the signals being obscured by steam and smoke beating down on the cab window. Col Mount wrote in his report: 'Though the wind was from a westerly direction at the time, it was probably not of sufficient velocity to preclude this possibility, having regard to the speed of the train, and the fact that the engine was steaming lightly on the falling gradient. But as Mr Anderson, the superintendent of motive power, said, Hudson (the driver) was a man who knew "every inch" of the road, and, as the distant signals are located in the only cutting in this neighbourhood, it is very difficult to believe that on a fine day, even though his view of the signals may have been temporarily obscured, he could have remained for nearly a minute under the wrong impression that he was still approaching them.

'There is no doubt, however, that Royal Scot engines suffer from this disadvantage, and though in consequence a driver would take precautions accordingly, and this feature heretofore has not had untoward results, it may be that on this occasion change of direction of the train on the curve accentuated the difficulty of vision.'

His recommendation that steps should be taken to test the effect of side-deflector plates, was accepted at once, and in a very short time all the Royal Scot class engines had been so equipped.

2

Speed: The Anglo-Scottish Breakthrough – and After

It is remarkable to recall for how long and how deeply the dislike of high speed running had persisted after the Race to the North in 1895. The alarming wreck of the 'Tourist' express at Preston, and bad accidents through excessive speed on curves at Shrewsbury, Grantham and Salisbury in 1905–6, all served to harden opinion both in the minds of the public and within the railway service that acceleration had gone far enough, despite the admonitions of enthusiasts who were continually emphasising the extent that we, in Great Britain, were being left behind in speed particularly by France and the USA. Maybe if competition with railways for long distance travel had come earlier affairs might not have remained as static as they were from the turn of the century up to 1914; and when pre-war speed was restored from the autumn of 1921 it was to the old standards that the schedules of long distance express trains were cut. When the record lengths of non-stop run were introduced on the principal trains between London and the Scottish cities of Edinburgh and Glasgow, the maintenance of minimum overall times of 8¼ hours made the point-to-point average speeds over most parts of the journeys considerably slower than had been necessary in 1914!

At first sight the early summer of 1932 would have seemed a strange time to introduce substantial accelerations of the Anglo-Scottish services, with the great slump in trade at its worst, and the economic measures taken by the National Government elected in the previous autumn having barely had time to make any impression. But although there was every need to effect all possible economies in operation, the enterprise of the LMS and LNER seized the mood of returning confidence in the country as a whole. Nevertheless, while reviewing the very striking improvements that came into effect on 2 May 1932, it must not be forgotten that the previous 8¼-hour schedules between London and Glasgow and Edinburgh were not the fastest that had been operated since the fateful year, 1896. It had then been agreed that the minimum should be 7¾ hours from King's Cross to Edinburgh, and 8 hours from Euston to both Glasgow and Edinburgh in deference to the longer mileage and heavier gradients of the

L & GRP, Courtesy David and Charles

7. A typical Midland shed interior: Lawrence Hill, Bristol in 1936. Engines, left to right, are: class 4P 0–6–0 no. 3858; three compounds, nos. 1026 and 1028, and one unidentified; class 3 'Belpaire' 4–4–0 no. 748; class 4P 0–6–0 no. 3875.

West Coast route. Before the war both routes had *night* trains running to these minimum times.

As from 2 May 1932 the overall time of the 'Royal Scot' from Euston to Glasgow was cut to 7 hours 55 minutes, and that of the 'Mid-day Scot' to 8 hours; in the period of the summer service the time of the 'Royal Scot' was cut further to 7 hours 40 minutes. These accelerated times were no more than a beginning, and the stepping stone to more general accelerations over the whole system. In keeping with East Coast improvements and to get it into Edinburgh ahead of the 'Flying Scotsman', the 9 am from St Pancras was accelerated by 20 minutes from London to Carlisle, including a non-stop run of 94 minutes over the 86.8 miles from Skipton, over Ais Gill summit. One of the sharpest of the new West Coast timings was that of 88 minutes start to stop over the 82.6 miles from Euston to Rugby, by the 'Mid-day Scot', with a load that usually topped the 500-ton mark.

By 1932 the 'tools for the job', to use that memorable phrase of Winston Churchill's, were certainly available. The original fifty Royal Scots had been reinforced by twenty more built at Derby, and construction had begun at Crewe with a batch of new Baby Scots replacing and taking the numbers of an equivalent number of small-boilered Claughtons. The Royal Scots, with the improved type of piston valves, were rising to absolutely top form, and I shall not forget my first run on one of the accelerated trains, when engine no. 6168, 'The Girl Guide' took a load of exactly 500 tons out of Euston on the 'Mid-day Scot'. She proved a particularly buxom wench, treating the fast schedule with complete disdain and arriving at Rugby 3½ minutes early. The average speed over the 46.3 miles from Tring Cutting box to Hillmorton was 68.5 mph including the notable minimum speeds with this load, of 59 mph at Roade and 57 mph at Kilsby Tunnel. Not long afterwards I had an even faster run behind no. 6115, 'Scots Guardsman', hauling the same load.

Author's Collection

8. The Royal Train climbing Shap hauled by Royal Scot class 4–6–0 no. 6119, 'Lancashire Fusilier'.

At the time of the May accelerations the LNER had set up a new record by booking the up Leeds breakfast car express, leaving Grantham at 9.40 am, over the 105.5 miles to King's Cross in 100 minutes start to stop. However, in the summer service the LMS went one better, taking what Cecil J. Allen described as the venturesome step of running the 5.25 pm from Liverpool to Euston over the 152.7 miles from Crewe to Willesden Junction in 142 minutes start to stop, an average of 64.5 mph. This train like its LNER speed rival was no lightweight, and a new category of load limits were laid down. Hitherto the principal express trains had been subject to what were known as 'special limit' loadings in which the accelerated Anglo-Scottish expresses were included, and for which the maximum tare weight for an unpiloted Royal Scot was 475 tons. The 'Liverpool Flyer', as it became unofficially known, was subject to 'XL Limits', which for a Royal Scot was 380 tons. On Friday nights, with one or two extra coaches, the train required double-heading from Crewe, usually with a Midland Compound. At first two engines, in specially good condition, one at Camden shed and one at Edge Hill were set aside for the working of this train. The two were no. 6105, 'Cameron Highlander', and no. 6140, 'Hector', and between them they provided a very high degree of reliability on this exacting service.

It will be appreciated that the setting aside of special engines for a particular duty was a complete negation of the former Midland operating principle that any engine in a usable condition should be able to work a duty within the loading classification laid down. But there was evidence that in other respects the old North Western traditions were coming to the fore again. The 'Liverpool Flyer' had a minimum load of just under 300 tons tare, and to enable it to be worked by other than Royal Scot locomotives on occasions the 'XL Limit' of loading was also specified for Class 5, and 5X engines, at that time covering the Claughton and rebuilt Claughton classes – the latter being the true rebuilds and also the Baby Scots. These limits were 300, and 340 tons respectively. But one

National Railway Museum

9. The first diesel shunting locomotive to work on the LMS, built by the Hunslet Engine Co. in 1932.

day in June 1933, when the load was 351 tons, and no Royal Scot was available a standard unrebuilt Claughton was put onto the job, one of the three named after LNWR men who won the V.C. in the First World War, no. 5967, 'L/Corpl. J. A. Christie V.C.' With such a load a pilot was provided, but this engine, a relatively new Class 2 4–4–0, proved of more hindrance than help and at Hillmorton Box, 2¼ miles south of Rugby, it failed altogether and had to be detached. The train engine then had 51 tons overload for the particular duty, and accordingly to the letter of the law the driver would have been entitled to demand a pilot, or else to run to slower point-to-point timings. He did neither. Instead he went 'all-out' for Willesden, and *regained* 2½ minutes on this fast schedule between Roade and the stop at Willesden Junction. A distance of 63.7 miles was covered at an average speed of 73.3 mph by this officially well-overloaded engine, and the maximum speed was 85 mph. This run, in relation to later achievements, is referred to in more detail in Chapter 7.

A spirit of enterprise and enthusiasm was spreading throughout the old North Western system, and the situation was fostered by the introduction of a periodical news-sheet, *On Time*, capitalising on the achievements and aspirations of all concerned with the running of the trains. It would be wrong to attribute all

F. R. Hebron, Rail Archive Stephenson

10. Two of the large-boilered Claughton class 4–6–0s fitted with Caprotti valve gear. Nos. 5908, 'Alfred Fletcher', and 5962 climb Camden bank with a Euston–Manchester express.

the credit to the old LNWR in this situation, because the Midland, Central, and Scottish Divisions became equally involved. The allocation of a number of the new Crewe-built Baby Scots to the Midland Division paved the way for some notable accelerations south of Nottingham and Leicester. I may add that until 1934 the Divisional Superintendent of Operation of the Midland was S. H. Fisher, otherwise a lifelong North Western man and aptly described as a human dynamo. He returned to Euston in 1934 as Assistant Chief Superintendent of Operation.

In view of the attention that had been aroused in 1929 by the appointment of A. F. Bound as Chief Signal and Telegraph Engineer, with a status unapproached by any other signalling officer on the British railways at that time, much interest and expectancy was shown towards the way future LMS signalling practice might develop. The immediate outcome was something of a surprise. As part of the programme for eliminating bottlenecks the track layout at Mirfield, on the former LYR main line, was to

National Railway Museum

11. The changing order on the Midland: interior of Kentish Town shed, showing two Baby Scots, nos. 6000 and 5545, between 0–4–4 tank engines nos. 1219 and 1321, and a Deeley compound, no. 1030.

be improved. This location had previously been something of a curiosity, for although this important route was quadruple tracked there were only two passenger lines through Mirfield station. This latter was of island type with bays at both ends, and the modernisation scheme was to provide two additional passenger running lines. There were major junctions at Heaton Lodge, 1.2 miles to the west, where the quadruple-tracked LNW line from Huddersfield joined, and Thornhill L&NW Junction, 1.6 miles to the east, where the direct line to Leeds diverged. The whole area seemed to offer an ideal opportunity for a central power signal-box, from which all working could be co-ordinated.

For a man who had been one of the foremost advocates of power signalling, Bound's treatment of the resignalling problem was surprising, and in retrospect somewhat reactionary. He retained the use of no less than *seven* signal-boxes, all with mechanical point operation, and although multiple aspect colour light signals were installed through the central area the signal aspects were of the 'speed' type, rather than of the conventional British geographical configurations. Bound had been to

F. R. Hebron, Rail Archive Stephenson

12. A strange combination, on an up express leaving Carlisle in 1931: an ex-LNW Precursor tank, no. 6813, piloting an unidentified ex-LYR 4-cylinder 4–6–0.

America and apparently had become completely converted to a system of signal aspects that was entirely novel on British railways. The Mirfield area included a plethora of crossover layouts, enabling trains to be switched from fast to slow lines and these were signalled in the American style, by displaying to the driver combinations of coloured lights that indicated high, medium and low speed, rather than the actual route that was to be taken. The major junctions at the outer ends retained semaphore signals geographically displayed for the diverging movements.

It was obviously a try-out, a guinea pig as it were, for the American system of aspects; and as such it was a complete breakaway from the system of multiple-aspect colour light signalling that had been evolved by the Committee of the

Institution of Railway Signal Engineers, of which Bound himself had been Chairman. It is true that at that time the problem of route indicating at junctions at which speed was high, or reasonably high, had not yet been solved, and the use of splitting aspects with colour light signal units closely abreast of each did not provide a satisfactory solution; but the American speed aspects would have involved British drivers learning a signalling code that would have been entirely new to them. Mirfield remained the only one of its kind in Great Britain.

At the British Industries Fair in February 1932 the Hunslet Engine Company, of Leeds, exhibited the first main line diesel shunting locomotive to be seen in Great Britain. It had an engine developing 150 horsepower and an entirely mechanical drive with a pre-selector gearbox. The final drive to the six wheels was by jackshaft and outside coupling rods. At the Fair the locomotive was on daily demonstration on a length of track outside and created much interest, so much so that the LMS agreed to put the locomotive on extended trial at the Hunslet Lane goods depot in Leeds. Sir Harold Hartley was interested because of the considerable economies in working that seemed likely, and he authorised a sum of £30,000 for experimenting on diesel shunting locomotives to determine the most suitable type. Three more diesels with mechanical transmission were purchased from Hunslet in 1934, but in the meantime Armstrong-Whitworth and the English Electric Company had entered the field, both with electrical transmission. Examples from both manufacturers were purchased for trial on the LMS.

It was at this time that the Electrical Engineer of the company, Lt-Col F. A. Cortez-Leigh, was due to retire. In choosing a successor it was perhaps no more than natural for Sir Harold Hartley to look for someone with a distinguished academic as well as an industrial background, in view of his conviction that improvement of the technology of all railway engineering was of supreme importance. C. E. Fairburn, Engineer and Manager of the Traction Department of the English Electric Company, seemed an ideal choice. He had joined the company, after distinguished war service, in 1919, to organise a railway electrification department, while before the war not only had he been a pupil of Sir Henry Fowler at Derby, but had been engaged on installation work for the Newport–Shildon electrified line of the North Eastern Railway. Before all this practical work on railways he had had a brilliant career at Oxford, where he took three Firsts – altogether a very impressive prelude to his appointment, in 1934, as Electrical Engineer of the LMS. He was well fitted to develop diesel and diesel-electric traction on the railway.

3
Vitalising the NCC

The Midland Railway through its steamer service via Heysham quietly nourished its tourist traffic to Northern Ireland. From the attractive photochrome views in its carriages we became familiar with the Giant's Causeway and the Glens of Antrim; but the Northern Counties Committee section of the railway went gently and unhurriedly on its way, with rolling stock that was of greater interest to the historian than to the connoisseur of modern practice. I must add, however, that the stock was well maintained and admirably fulfilled the modest tasks required of it. There was little change in the early years of the LMS. The circumstances leading to the first step in the chain of events that transformed the NCC from near-mediocrity to one of the most enterprising and efficient sections of the LMS was, oddly enough, the ill-wind that brought stagnation and grievous unemployment in the heavy industries of Belfast, and which led the Government of Northern Ireland to ask the railways to consider the undertaking of works to provide some relief.

The NCC had inherited from the Belfast and Northern Counties Railway a track layout on its main line that for sheer awkwardness in operation bid fair to rival the famous situation on the Great Southern and Western at Limerick Junction. No farther out of Belfast than Greenisland trains for the North Atlantic coast and Londonderry had to reverse direction and start afresh up the steep gradient towards Antrim. It was a time-consuming business, and it precluded any chance of providing smart services in the modern style between Belfast and the popular resort of Portrush. The offer of Government loans at advantageous rates of interest gave the opportunity to untie this age-old Gordian Knot, and plans were made for a new loop line that would permit direct running between Belfast and the north. They involved some notable viaduct construction north of White Abbey, as shown on the accompanying map, not the least interesting feature of which is that one viaduct, that carrying the down Larne line, dives clean under the taller structure carrying the Londonderry line. In the interests of providing maximum employment the viaducts were designed and the work organised to be carried out almost entirely with unskilled labour, recruited directly from local employment offices. The speed and success with which the viaducts were built was a remarkable tribute to W. K. Wallace, practically his last work in Ireland. The work was carried to completion under the supervision of R. L. McIlmoyle.

The viaduct carrying the Londonderry line was the largest of its kind carrying a railway anywhere in the British Isles. The three central

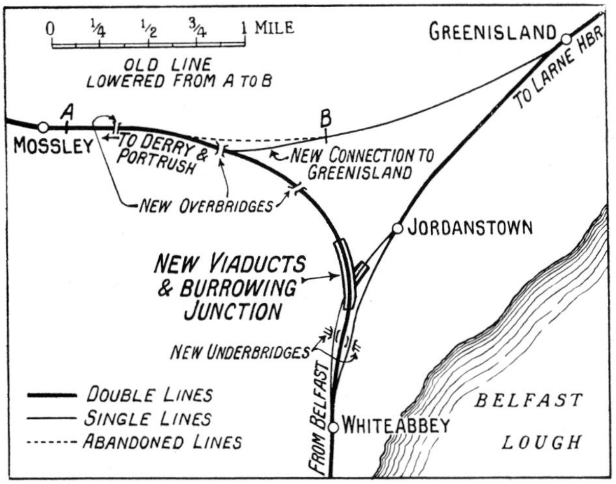

By courtesy of The Railway Magazine

Arrangement of new viaducts and burrowing junction at Greenisland.

arches each have a span of 89 ft and the maximum height is 70 ft above ground level. In the construction of these arches a slender steel framework was built to support the shuttering, instead of the more usual practice of building up a wooden framework from ground level. This steel framework took the form of a number of sickle-shaped trusses, on to the top of which was fixed the temporary woodwork. The finished faces of the concrete were left as cast, and by a careful arrangement of the shuttering boards the marks left gave the viaducts an attractive appearance, quite unlike the dead flat effect of concrete work. The two viaducts together, one passing underneath the other, produced one of the most distinctive and original pieces of railway civil engineering in these islands. The work was started in January 1931 and was completed at the end of 1933.

In February 1931 Major Malcolm S. Speir was appointed Manager and Secretary of the NCC, a man of outstanding energy and enthusiasm whom I came to know well through various assignments in Northern Ireland. His pre-war railway service had been on the Midland and Caledonian Railways, and after more than four years active service in the Royal Engineers, entirely in France, and a brief return to the Caledonian afterwards, in 1923 he was appointed Assistant General Superintendent, Northern Division, LMS. Many tales were told of his dynamic and ubiquitous tenure of that high office. He seemed to be everywhere at once! On crossing to Ireland he continued in the same style, often astonishing his chief officers by his wide grasp of every railway activity. But he had a charming personality and was a source of inspiration to the entire staff.

It was not long before he was taking advantage of the new direct line at Greenisland, by making a complete re-casting of the main line passenger train service. North of Ballymena the main line both to Londonderry and to Portrush was single-tracked throughout, and the passing loops were equipped for mechanical exchanging of tablets on the Manson system, with which, of course, he was fully familiar from his work in Scotland. But in the new accelerated schedules he was planning he did not want the handicap of any slowing, however slight, while tablets were exchanged, and the track layouts and signalling at the loops were re-arranged to permit full speed running in both directions by non-stopping trains. Instead of the usual layout of 'down' and 'up' lines through the loops one line was set aside for non-stopping trains in both directions, and the track alignment made capable of taking maximum line speed. Stopping trains used the second track through the loop with curved turnouts at each end. Throughout the main line, single and double track alike, interlocking of the starting signals was installed, so that they could not be cleared unless the train had been accepted by the signal box in advance. The way was then clear for major acceleration of the train service.

John Edgington

13. A picturesque view of the Greenisland viaducts looking north, showing the single track of the down Larne line (centre) emerging from its underpass beneath the main line to Portrush and Londonderry. The up line from Larne (right) is the only one not to pass over one of the new concrete viaducts.

On the main line through to Londonderry, on which the NCC was in mild competition with the Great Northern for through traffic, no very marked improvements were made. It was Portrush, at the end of the short branch from Coleraine, that was made the principal target, with three expresses daily booked to cover the 65½ miles from Belfast in 80 minutes, inclusive of one intermediate stop. This was no easy run because, although the loads were not heavy by LMS standards in England, the route included some awkward gradients and not all the station and junction layouts allowed for uninterrupted high speed. The ascent from the shores of Belfast Lough to Ballyclare Junction included 3 miles of 1 in 76½ over the new Greenisland loop line, preceeded by a mile of 1 in 102, and one would be doing well to cover the 8.2 miles from Belfast to Ballyclare Junction in much under 14 minutes.

Until 1933 no larger locomotives than small superheater 4–4–0s were available, based generally on the Midland Class 2 design, but with 6 ft instead of 7 ft diameter coupled wheels.

H. C. Casserley

14. Two-cylinder compound 2–4–0 no. 57, 'Galgorm Castle', leaving Cookstown Junction on a Belfast–Cookstown train on 20 June 1938.

15. One of the County class 4–4–0s, rebuilt from a class B light compound: no. 60, 'County Donegal', at Londonderry on 24 June 1937.

H. C. Casserley

Author

16. One of the four superheater 4–4–0s introduced by Bowman Malcolm in 1914, no. 73, at Londonderry. They were the first non-compound locomotives built for the line since 1876.

These engines were new in 1924, but from 1926 onwards Mr W. K. Wallace had begun a systematic renewal of the stud of 2-cylinder Worsdell–Von Borries compounds, built by Bowman Malcolm during his long innings as locomotive engineer; and when I first visited the NCC section, in 1935, there were only a few left as compounds. Many had been rebuilt to correspond with the U2 4–4–0s that had been built new in 1924, mostly by the North British Locomotive Company. A number, however, had smaller boilers, but nevertheless did much excellent work. At a time when nearly all LMS passenger locomotives in Great Britain were painted black, and often none too clean, it was a delight to see the NCC engines all in Midland red and beautifully turned out.

In the early months of 1933 there had been a lengthy railway strike in Northern Ireland. Until then the NCC still had three narrow gauge lines in operation with passenger services. These were the Ballymena and Larne, the Parkmore line, which ran from Ballymena into the high country that formed the immediate hinterland to the Antrim coast, and the Ballycastle Railway. On the first two the passenger services were not restarted but were replaced by bus services, also run by the NCC. From the railway operating point of view the Ballymena and

Author

17. Rebuilt 4–4–0 no. 87, 'Queen Alexandra', originally one of the 'heavy compounds', no. 63, and bearing the same name. The latter engine still in the 'invisible green' livery of pre-grouping days was not rebuilt until 1936.

Larne line had been particularly interesting in that a narrow-gauge boat express was run in connection with the cross-channel steamer service to Stranraer, covering the 25 steeply graded miles between Ballymena and Larne Harbour in a few minutes over the even hour. Some very comfortable bogie carriages were used on these trains, which were transferred to the Ballycastle Railway, when the passenger service on that line was restored after the strike.

In 1908 the Ballycastle Railway had taken delivery from Kitsons, of Leeds, of two rather clumsy looking 4–4–2 tank engines, but after the strike these were transferred to the Ballymena and Larne line for goods working, and their places taken by two of Bowman Malcolm's beautiful little 2–4–2 compound tank engines. These, of course, had outside cylinders of odd sizes; but they were splendid little machines and had a good turn of speed. When I travelled on the Ballycastle line in 1935 there were two of them stationed there, each working the entire service on alternate days. The six engines of the class were built at intervals between 1892 and 1920, all to the same design. The two original engines were built by Beyer Peacock & Co., but all the others were built at the Belfast works of the NCC. Like the broad gauge engines of the committee they were painted Midland red, and kept looking very smart.

Easily the most remarkable of NCC locomotives in the 1930s, were the 2–6–0s introduced in 1933, ready for the accelerated services

Author

18. Up goods train at Ballymena, hauled by 2–6–0 locomotive no. 95, 'The Braid'.

made possible by the completion of the Greenisland loop line. The design was based to some extent upon the Derby 2–6–4 tank engines of the 2300 class. There were eventually nine of these engines, having 6 ft diameter coupled wheels and cylinders 19 ins diameter by 26 ins stroke, and what contributed mainly to their remarkable freedom in running and high thermal efficiency was the provision of very large diameter piston valves, and long valve travel. I had the privilege of making a number of runs on their footplates. The ideal method of locomotive working, with short cut-offs and a wide open regulator, was carried to an extent that I had never previously seen, and was later equalled only on some trials made when the Royal Scots were rebuilt during the Second World War. Working with cut-offs as short as 7, and even 5 per cent, became everyday practice on the Belfast–Portrush 80-minute expresses. With the normal loads of these trains, however, a little less than 200 tons, the 4–4–0 engines could also keep very good time, if a 2–6–0 was not available.

Smart working was not confined to the Portrush trains. The boat expresses to and from Larne Harbour, allowed 30 minutes for the 24.3 mile run from Belfast, were very sharply timed in relation to the restrictions of the route. The line was single-tracked from Whitehead to Larne, and although tablets could be exchanged at speed the curves round the coastal section particularly at Magheramorne required some restraint, and there was a concluding heavy slack through Larne Town. The boat train connecting with the morning steamer to Stranraer, which provided a daytime service from Belfast to London with a through carriage from Stranraer to Euston, attached to the up 'Mid-day Scot' at Carlisle, had what appeared to be a very sharp connection with the up North Atlantic Express in Belfast – only 5 minutes – until one learned that the same set of coaches was used for both trains. The fresh engine, usually one of the largest 4–4–0s backed on to what had been the rear of the train.

Larne Harbour itself was also the scene of some very smart transfer working between train and boat. By use of a belt conveyor the transhipment of luggage and mails was developed into a fine art, characteristic of all operations developed by Major Speir. The schedule time between arrival of the train and departure of the steamer was *8 minutes*, and no concession was given at times of exceptional holiday traffic. I have seen the train arrive from Belfast with a ten-coach load, packed to standing with passengers, and still the boat was dispatched in not a second over the allotted 8 minutes. The belt conveyor was carried alongside one of the tracks, level with the carriage floors, and then inclined upwards so as to pass high and clear over the landing stage. The outward end of the conveyor consisted of a movable arm which could either be lowered onto the deck of the ship, or be hoisted up out of the way when not in use.

Although on the many trips I made to Northern Ireland in 1935–6 I was in search of slick modern operation, which was the hallmark of all Major Speir's activities, I could not resist seeking out the remaining 2-cylinder compounds of Bowman Malcolm's design. In all there were five of them – three 2–4–0s one 6 ft 4–4–0 and one 7 ft 4–4–0. Three out of the five were stationed at Cookstown, and one day I went down from Belfast to Magherafelt on the footplate of the 'Galgorm Castle', a 2–4–0 rebuilt with a larger boiler. To ride this sporting little engine at 65 mph was an entertaining experience! But there was a significance about that run that went far beyond the 'fun' of riding an historic engine. Those old compounds and their crews had to work up to the exacting standards expected of everyone on the NCC. The spirit and the sense of pride in the job was everywhere, and everyone delighted to have a visitor with them, and to display to him their own particular craft and skill.

4
Stanier: His Mandate and Impact

At the time Stanier took up his appointment as Chief Mechanical Engineer, in January 1932, there was just ending in the *Railway Magazine* a long serial article listing in complete detail the present-day locomotives of the LMS. It had run for just over two years, and was based on official information that gave the position in October 1929. While it was true that there had been changes in the two years that followed, by withdrawal of obsolete units, the general position, as revealed in those articles, is enough to show the immensity of the task facing Stanier in carrying out his mandate for complete modernisation of the locomotive stock. In round figures the totals were, LNWR 3,200; Midland, including those taken over from the Tilbury, 2,900; LYR 1,309; North Staffordshire, 150; Furness, 90; Caledonian 950; G&SWR 450; Highland 130. Of these, only the compounds and Class 2 4–4–0s of the Midland, together with the 4F 0–6–0s could be regarded as anything approaching standards, in that many more of each class had been built since grouping. Of the new designs introduced since 1923, the Royal Scots, the Horwich Moguls, the 2–6–4 tanks and the Garratts were stalwarts on which reliance would have to be placed for many years, while the Baby Scots seemed to be the latest 'hope of the side'.

Good though they were, however, Stanier's first reconnaisances around his new command convinced him that, from his nigh-lifelong experience on the Great Western, none of them would measure up to the demands of accelerated service, with maximum utilisation of every locomotive. Both Royal and Baby Scots showed good economy in respect of coal consumption in relation to work done; but both were prone to casualties, as they then existed. An entirely new range of locomotives was decided upon to implement a policy of 'scrap and build'. But while Stanier had his almost unrivalled experience of Great Western locomotives to work upon, supplemented by a large wooden box full of blueprints of vital parts, urgency was the veritable watchword of his mandate. He had the outstanding benefit of having grown up, as it were, amid Churchward's great scheme of standardisation on the Great Western. However, compared with the comparative leisure of Churchward's development, with plenty of reliable and acceptable older units to bear the heat and burden of the day while the new designs were being evolved,

Author's Collection

19. A group at Crewe in 1933, in front of the first Pacific, no. 6200, 'The Princess Royal'. Left to right: H. Chambers, Chief Draughtsman; R. A. Riddles, Locomotive Assistant to CME; S. J. Symes, Chief Stores Superintendent; W. A. Stanier, Chief Mechanical Engineer; H. P. M. Beames, Deputy Chief Mechanical Engineer; F. A. Lemon, Works Manager, Crewe.

Stanier had to design new locomotives that would supersede existing engines of Class 4 and Class 5 capacity on all parts of the line, and get them into traffic quickly.

Furthermore, he had to take the measure of staffs nurtured on the old railways, all with their own traditions, and to assess the capabilities of the main works at Crewe, Derby, Horwich and St Rollox. New locomotives were wanted so urgently that large contracts had to be placed with the private locomotive builders, particularly the North British Locomotive Company and the Vulcan Foundry. It was a programme that could have gone disastrously wrong, with so many different interests and so many different people involved. That it did not was in a very large measure due to Stanier himself. He was in no sense an engine designer, but he was an altogether outstanding workshop man. He was even more than that, in being an extraordinarily shrewd judge of character and a great leader of men. In handing out those Swindon blueprints he did not insist on their being slavishly copied; he was ready to see the points raised by drawing office and works' staffs that had a wealth of experience of their own. And so,

Author's Collection

20. The second Pacific, no. 6201 (before naming), fitted with indicator shelters for test running.

within a very short time, every drawing office and every works on the LMS was solidly behind him.

It was not all plain sailing. That some of the awkward situations – inevitable in the circumstances – did not get a great deal worse was due to Stanier's choice of his assistants, and to the unswerving loyalty they gave to him. At first he had taken the existing personnel situation as it was, but in 1933 he brought R. A. Riddles to Euston, to be Locomotive Assistant to the CME. Riddles once described this appointment to me, in his characteristically witty style as 'political agent to the CME'! While Stanier's department was solidly behind him, there were still 'dark areas' on the LMS and one high officer, who ought to have known better, consistently referred to him as 'that bloody watchmaker'. Presumably he had heard of Churchward's use of the term 'watchmakers' work' to describe the running gear of the de Glehn compound 4–4–2, 'La France', not in any derogatory sense, but in praise of the machinery. But on the LMS in the 1930s this leading light in the anti-Stanier faction seized upon it in entirely the wrong sense.

Riddles was quick to sense that this minority, entirely outside the CME's department, was ready to pounce upon any shortcomings of the new locomotives and blow them up in an attempt to undermine Stanier. There were certainly some opportunities in the years 1933 and 1934. The Baby Scots were proving so successful that many more were built to replace the small-boilered Claughtons, and attention was first directed to the new 'super' main line engine that would not only be capable of working through between Euston and Glasgow, but would need only a short layover between northbound and southbound runs. The answer was a Pacific version of the Great Western King, of

F. R. Hebron, Rail Archive Stephenson

21. One of the first Jubilee class 5X 3-cylinder 4–6–0s, built by the North British Locomotive Co., no. 5574, yet to be named 'India', near Rugby with a train for Manchester in 1936.

exactly the same tractive effort but with a much larger boiler and a grate area of 45 sq. ft. Two of these enormous engines were built at Crewe in 1933, no. 6200, 'The Princess Royal', and no. 6201, 'Princess Elizabeth'. The intention at first was to use them on the 'Royal Scot' train, one in each direction daily between Euston and Glasgow. But at first it did not quite work out that way.

Stanier began by using the Great Western principle of a medium degree of superheat. In seeking to achieve maximum thermal efficiency with a simple engine, in competition with a compound, Churchward adopted a degree of superheat that provided for none to be thrown away in the exhaust. After expansion the steam would be back to the saturated condition. This was an ideal theoretical balance, but it depended on almost perfect steaming, with boiler pressure constantly up to maximum. If pressure fell to any extent by the time it was expanded you finished with wet steam. Great Western engine crews had, over long years, been trained to work with maximum boiler pressure. If there was a drop to about 200 lbs per sq. in. an engine would be stigmatised as 'not steaming'. Things had been very different on the LMS. Ever since Bowen Cooke had achieved such remarkable results with the George the Fifth class 4–4–0s

• *Author's Collection*

22. One of the ever-famous 'Black Five' 4–6–0s, one of the earliest batch built at Crewe, no. 5005.

and their successors, a high degree of superheat had been used, and in riding Royal Scots I saw the pressure allowed to seesaw up and down in the most nonchalant way, with no effect on the performance, even with trains loaded to maximum tonnage on 'special limit' timings.

But there was more to it than the degree of superheat behind the early deficiencies of the first Stanier Pacifics. Even with good coal they were not free steamers. The boiler proportions and the draughting were not ideal, and things were not made easier by those exceptionally long through workings. I shall always remember the remark of a very good Carlisle fireman regarding no. 6201: 'The Glasgow boys come in and say "she won't steam" and you've 300 miles to go, non stop!' Riddles strove might and main to keep the flag flying for Stanier. In his autobiography R. C. Bond tells of a sharp rebuke he received over a repair to 6201. The anti-Stanier faction was ready to seize upon any defect, and instructions were issued from Euston that neither of the Pacifics were to be taken into the works for repair if the job could be done on shed. At Crewe relations between

F. R. Hebron, Rail Archive Stephenson

23. Stanier 3-cylinder suburban tank engine, of class introduced in 1934 and built at Derby. No. 2501 is leaving Elstree with the 3.10 pm train from St Pancras to St Albans.

the running people and the works were close and cordial, and a case occurred where a defect could be rectified much quicker and the engine back in traffic by taking it into the works, rather than by attending to it with less suitable tools in the shed. Bond agreed to do it in the works and got a 'rocket' from Riddles for his pains! For sometime afterwards I wondered how it was that the publicity department so readily arranged a footplate pass for me on no. 6200 in the early months of 1934, when the difficulties were at their worst, at a time when such a privilege, to anyone outside the railway service, was as grudgingly granted as hereditary honours! I have several times told the inside story of how Laurie Earl and his fireman, with a little indirect assistance from me, coaxed the reluctantly steaming engine through on the long non-stop run from Carlisle to Euston, with a 500-ton train, and how the *Star* newspaper splashed headlines FOUR MINS. EARLY to the feature article I subsequently wrote. It formed a valuable independent boost to the 'Back up Stanier' campaign being waged by Riddles, though it was many years later before I became aware of the modest part I had been able to play, through the luck of riding with an outstanding driver.

By the time that article of mine was published the first examples of the next Stanier standard

T. G. Hepburn, Rail Archive Stephenson

24. One of the later Pacifics of the Princess Royal class, no. 6208, 'Princess Helena Victoria', at Rugby.

designs were coming into traffic, and the first 3-cylinder 5X 4–6–0 of the Jubilee class did not improve the already delicate situation. These engines were intended to be the equivalent of the Baby Scots, but with the Swindon taper boiler. Low superheat or not, however, they just would not steam! Naturally this did not endear them to men of the old North Western, who were quickly making unkind comparisons with the Baby Scots, and not least with the old Crewe stalwarts on which, of course, reliance was still being placed for a considerable proportion of the Western Division express passenger workings. Even when they were steaming reasonably well their basic coal consumption was disconcertingly higher than that of the Baby Scots. Drastic action was needed, all the more so in that engines of the class were arriving in considerable numbers from contractors' works. While the troubles were being diagnosed and plans for remedial action made Riddles arranged for as many of them as possible to be allocated to the Midland Division, where it was hoped that they would show sufficient superiority over the existing engines as to be appreciated as an improvement. Even this did not entirely work out as planned. I remember going down to Leeds one night on the 6.15 pm from St Pancras, with a load of no more than eight coaches, a task that any self-respecting compound would have made light of, and our Jubilee barely held its own. I spoke to the driver at Leeds and he blamed it on the superheater, which, he averred 'wouldn't heat water, let alone steam!'

Fortunately the 'Black Fives', the first of which followed the Jubilees into traffic, were almost right from the start, and although they were much improved afterwards they immediately gave a good account of themselves. Then also, while the most urgent steps were being taken to get the Jubilees right, an entirely new boiler was designed for the Pacifics. The way in which this differed from the original one shows how readily Stanier was willing to adapt himself to LMS conditions, and to take full advantage of the experience and advice of the able men on his staff. All ideas of a moderate degree of superheat were thrown to the winds. The original 16-element type was replaced by one of 32-elements; the length between the tube plates was reduced by 1 ft 6 ins and the diameter of the small tubes increased. The effectiveness of the new design was shown by a spectacular run on the up 'Liverpool Flyer' on 27 June 1935, when the 152.7 miles from Crewe to Willesden Junction were covered in 129½ minutes start to stop, instead of the 142-minute schedule, and that with a gross load behind the tender of 475 tons. A few days later engine no. 6200 made an equally brilliant test run from Crewe to Glasgow and back. Ten more Pacifics having the improved boiler were built at Crewe later in 1935, and the magnificent performances of these engines in the ensuing winter of 1935–6, together with the greatly improved work of the Jubilees set the seal on the first phase of the Stanier regime. Its impact was becoming tremendous.

The summer of 1935 was also signalised by two important changes in personnel in the CME's department. R. A. Riddles, who from 1933 had been Locomotive Assistant to the CME, was made Principal Assistant, taking the title that Stanier himself had held on the Great Western. At the same time it was felt that new blood was needed in the headquarters drawing office at Derby, where Herbert Chambers of the Midland had reigned for so long. Chambers was not quite due for retirement, and it was typical of Stanier's kindly nature that in replacing him at Derby he made an appointment that kept him in the centre of affairs – Locomotive and Personal Assistant to the CME, at Euston. At Derby T. F. Coleman was appointed Chief Draughtsman – a very happy and successful choice. Coleman had been on the North Staffordshire Railway from 1906 until Grouping, and he remained at Stoke as Chief Draughtsman until 1926, when he was transferred to Horwich. In 1933 he had been appointed Assistant Chief Draughtsman of the LMS, based at Crewe, and head of the drawing office there. From 1935, it was under his direction that design work for the brilliant second stage of the Stanier regime was carried out, at Derby.

5 Developments in Many Spheres

While the locomotive department held the centre of the stage, as it were, in its spectacular progress in the mid-1930s, it is remarkable in what a diversity of directions the drive and enterprise of the LMS management began to show itself. It seemed that nothing was being left untouched, where increased operational efficiency and reduced running costs could be realised. There was an interesting case at Fleetwood, which, because of the rationalisation of Anglo–Irish shipping services, had lost its one-time role as a packet station. The fish traffic there remained important, but the LMS had a two-way interest in this – not only taking the fish to markets, but in coaling the trawlers. This latter had hitherto been a somewhat primitive labour intensive operation, but in 1937 a new, fully mechanised, coal handling plant was brought into service, by which six trawlers could be coaled simultaneously. Loaded coal wagons were hauled by electrically operated capstans up to one of the three tiplers, in which the coal was transferred to belt conveyors, which in turn delivered to telescopic boom conveyors mounted on a travelling bridge structure. Each of the conveyors had a capacity of 200 tons per hour. It was a notable example of a fully integrated, mechanical handling plant, for which Mr Stanier's staff were responsible for the specifications.

From bunkering facilities it is a natural step to the ships operated by the LMS. The fleet operating on the Firth of Clyde has always been a source of great interest to enthusiasts of the 'narrow seas' and in 1936 a fine new turbine steamer, the 'Marchioness of Graham', was put onto the run from Ardrossan to the Isle of Arran. She was a replacement for the old paddle steamer, 'Jupiter', of the former Glasgow and South Western fleet. All steamers plying on the Firth of Clyde had to be equipped for mass transportation and the 'Marchioness of Graham', although having a gross tonnage of no more than 585 had accommodation for no less than 1,332 passengers and crew. She had four decks, boat, promenade, main, and lower, and a service speed of 16–17 knots. She was built by the Fairfield Shipbuilding and Engineering Co. Ltd of Govan. At the time of her inaugural cruise, Sir Arthur Rose, a director of the LMS, made the point that with then-modern travel facilities it was possible for a person to dine and go to a theatre in London, leave Euston by the 'Night Scot' and have lunch in Arran next day.

John Edgington

25. Launch of the turbine steamer *Marchioness of Graham* from the yard of the Fairfield Shipbuilding and Engineering Co., on the Clyde.

The LMS inherited from the Furness Railway a picturesque fleet of steamers plying on Windermere and Coniston lakes many of which were of great historical interest. The older ones had locomotive type boilers and valve gear, and made their way up and down Windermere to a puffing exhaust. One of these was the 'Teal' on which, as a boy, I made many journeys. In July 1936 the LMS took delivery of a new 'Teal', a diesel-engined vessel built by Vickers-Armstrong Ltd at Barrow. As the outflow from Lake Windermere is very far from navigable, the vessel had to be conveyed in sections by rail to Lakeside, where a special slipway was constructed, and re-erected thereon. Like the Clyde steamers the launches on Lake Windermere are by tradition designed to carry passengers in bulk. The main deck of the new 'Teal' extended to the full length of the vessel, while on the lower deck were separate tea rooms and lounges for first and third-class passengers. Her gross tonnage was 230, and accommodation was provided for 800 passengers. The speed was 11 knots.

In 1936 notable progress was being made in the introduction of diesel-electric locomotives for shunting. Although at that time little, if any consideration was being given to the use of such locomotives for main line work their use for shunting was an attractive proposition, in that the units were available for continuous duty, for virtually indefinite periods and they involved no stand-by losses when not actually at work. Following earlier experience with diesel-mechanical locomotives the LMS ordered twenty diesel-electrics of 350 bhp, ten from Armstrong Whitworth and ten from the English Electric Co Ltd. The latter proved

John Edgington

26. The paddle steamer, *Marchioness of Lorne*, approaching Gourock.

important in the history of motive power development on the LMS because they became the prototypes of a large standard class of shunting locomotives, all using a 6-cylinder, 350 horsepower English Electric diesel engine. The original batch of 1936 had two nose-suspended motors, with single reduction gear drive, and a maximum tractive effort of 30,000 lbs. In the later versions the tractive effort was increased, first to 33,000 lbs and then to 35,000. When first put into service in the yard at Crewe South Sidings they averaged about 146 locomotive and 138 engine-hours a week, utilisations respectively of 87 and 82.2 per cent.

When studying the activities of a great railway one could imagine that little thought might be given to the road motor department. The vehicles would be seen out and about, but the need for a major organisation behind their movements might not be readily apparent. When, however, it is noted that in 1936 the LMS operated no fewer than 3,287 motor vehicles and 2,130 trailers over the entire extent of the system, it will be appreciated that a first-class organisation would be needed to service, maintain and repair such a fleet efficiently. And this work was undertaken in the same thoroughgoing manner as with all other activities. In England, while the headquarters of the Road

BBC Hulton Picture Library

27. Representatives of the growing fleet of LMS diesel shunters, posed in Crewe south sidings in 1936.

F. R. Hebron, Rail Archive Stephenson

28. A relic of earlier days, in the 1930s: a local train from Bangor to Holyhead leaving the Britannia tubular bridge, hauled by one of the Webb 0–6–2 'coal tanks'.

Motor Engineer of the company was at Euston, the routine maintenance of the fleet was decentralised into five sections, each in charge of a District Road Motor Engineer, each having its own main workshops for heavy repairs and routine overhauls. The five districts were:

(a) London, extending northward to Cambridge and Northampton, and eastwards to Shoeburyness
(b) Birmingham, the Midlands, South Wales to Swansea, and the Somerset and Dorset Line
(c) Blackburn, Lancashire west of Manchester, North Wales, Furness district and Cumberland
(d) Manchester, East Lancashire, Midland lines to Derby, Nottingham and Lincoln
(e) Bradford, the West Riding of Yorkshire

In Scotland the necessary work was done by the Motive Power Superintendent, on behalf of the Road Motor Engineer of the company. The general supervision of the fleet, and the programming for repairs was organised on the same precision and flowline principles as for repair of locomotives. It may be added that V. R. Bowen Cooke, son of the former CME of the LNWR, served his entire service with the company in the Road Motor department, ultimately, in 1946, becoming Assistant Road Motor Engineer.

It was one of the curiosities and anomalies of the grouping arrangements that little or no provision was made for rationalising train services in many areas. The complicated situation that remained was nowhere more apparent than around Liverpool, and in the Wirral peninsula. The accompanying map shows that while the former Wirral Railway became part of the LMS

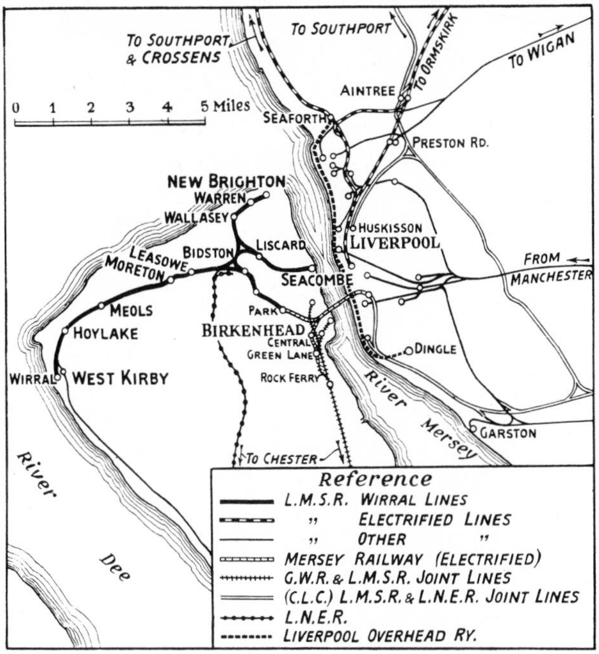

By courtesy of The Railway Magazine

LMSR lines in the Wirral Peninsula. The whole of the former Wirral Railway (shown by a thick black line) was converted to electric traction, except the branch to Seacombe, and through services from Liverpool Central station to West Kirby and New Brighton provided via the Mersey Railway.

it was isolated entirely from the parent system, and made physical contact with a GW & LMS Joint Line, with a remote branch of the LNER (ex Great Central) and with the electrified Mersey Railway, which strange to say remained independent. Under the Railways (Agreement) Act 1935, the LMS and the Mersey Railway arranged for a through service of electric trains from the Wirral stations to Liverpool Central, following electrification by the LMS of all the former Wirral Railway, except the branch to Seacombe. The system of electrification was to be third rail, at 650 volt d.c. as on the Mersey Railway. The new LMS electric stock was to be pooled with the existing Mersey Railway equipment. This latter was somewhat spartan in its amenities. Being an underground line no heating was provided in the trains and seats were devoid of upholstery. To render them suitable for running out to West Kirby or to New Brighton these deficiencies were to be made good.

While electrification, where the high capital cost could be justified, was by that time recognised as the ideal form of traction for commuter services round large cities, and the diesel-electric was rapidly becoming favoured for shunting, the relatively low overall efficiency of the steam locomotive, and the rising price of coal was constantly giving rise to thoughts of alternatives to the basic Stephensonian reciprocating locomotive. On the LNER Gresley had built an experimental compound locomotive with a Yarrow, marine-type, water tube boiler, and Sir Henry Fowler having tried the Ljungstrom condensing turbine, of Swedish origin, had built his ill-fated 'Fury', with a name that had a poignant significance. In 1932, however, a non-condensing turbine locomotive had been put into service on the Grangesberg–Oxelosung Railway in Sweden, and was giving excellent results, and at the invitation of Dr H. L. Guy, then Chief Turbine Engineer of Metropolitan-Vickers, Stanier went over to Sweden to see the locomotive at work. He was sufficiently impressed to begin to collaborate with Dr Guy in the design of a non-condensing turbine version of the Princess Royal class Pacific. Thus the celebrated Turbomotive, no. 6202, came into being.

As a motive power unit there is no doubt that this locomotive was a great success. It performed the same duties as the ordinary Pacifics with ease and efficiency. It was, of course, under close observation all the time, and could not be released to the running department for use as an ordinary traffic machine, though it

BBC Hulton Picture Library

29. An interesting picture in the paint shop at Crewe on 14 September 1934, showing new Jubilee class 4–6–0s nos. 5624 and 5625 being finished alongside the veteran 2–2–2 'Cornwall'.

worked in the regular links, and did a good deal of satisfactory, revenue-earning service, principally between Euston and Liverpool. I had some excellent runs behind it on the heavy and fast down 'Merseyside Express', one of them the fastest I ever experienced on that train. But up to 1939 the economy in basic fuel consumption over that of the Princess Royal class engines was neither sufficient to justify the costs of constant invigilation nor the time out of service for curing the inevitable teething troubles with so novel a motive power unit; and no. 6202 remained a 'one-off'. On a series of dynamometer car test runs on the 'Royal Scot' train, made in 1936, the locomotive was pitted against two standard Pacifics, nos 6210 and 6212, with very heavy trains. On three runs no. 6202 returned a coal consumption of 2.86, 3.14 and 2.91 lbs per drawbar horsepower hour, while two runs with no. 6212 gave 3.04 and 3.10 lbs. On her one test run, however, no. 6210 gave a figure equal to the best turbine result, 2.86 lbs, so there did not seem to be any

J. N. Hall, Rail Archive Stephenson

30. The magnificent Stanier experiment into turbine propulsion. The great 4–6–2 no. 6202 on arrival at Euston with an up Liverpool express.

significant difference from this series of tests. Later experience with this locomotive and the reasons for its ultimate demise are referred to in the final volume of this series.

The increasingly exacting demands of railway management, engineering and operation, against the continuing economic and financial stringency in the country as a whole led Sir Josiah Stamp and his Vice-Presidents to the view that the old methods of training railwaymen for the more senior posts, rising from the humblest ranks, gathering experience on the way, was no longer adequate. In the mid-1930s, as had been the case on the majority of the old railways of Britain, a man's success was often due to his chance training under a first-class senior officer, at any rate as far as the non-engineering branches of the service were concerned. It was remarkable nevertheless that most of the chief executive officers had risen to prominence purely from the display of ability in the ordinary day to day tasks, rather than from any system of organised study. There were no textbooks, nor courses of study at evening classes from which a man could learn the principles of operation.

So there was evolved the idea of a Staff College, to be set up at Derby. It was the first ever to be introduced on a British railway, and to accommodate it a splendid new building was designed by the company's architect, Mr W. H. Hamlyn. The college was to be residential and to provide for fifty members of the staff selected from all grades. The period of training envisaged was anything from a fortnight upwards. In the railway industry it had come to be realised that a great loss of valuable knowledge and experience had occurred through its not being recorded before men retired from the service, and one of the objects of the staff college was to ensure that textbooks should be prepared incorporating the best practices. By this means it was intended that the non-engineering work of the railway should be put on the same footing as the engineering, and that knowledge should be recorded and be available to every member of the staff. Known eventually as the School of Transport it was opened in July 1938.

6
The Drive for Punctuality: 'On Time'

It was Sir Richard Moon, during the thirty years of his great Chairmanship of the London and North Western Railway, who used to interview all senior officers on their appointment to positions of high responsibility, and impress upon them, as gentlemen, the nigh-sanctity of performing what they had promised in the way of service to the public. And in his view the passenger timetable was a promise! So also were many other business arrangements, but the passenger timetable was the prime instrument of public relations. That was one reason why he resisted acceleration of trains. It would be more difficult to keep one's promise. There is no doubt that taken all round punctuality on the LMS had not been good in its first ten years, and in the modern era the machinery of operation, and the diversity of interests and skills involved had become far too complex for success to be achieved merely by top-level exhortations to senior officers. It was not only a question of dealing with main line express trains – the kind of services noticed in the 'British Locomotive Practice and Performance' feature in the *Railway Magazine* – it was every train, down to the humblest branch line local.

The formula that was applied in 1935, under the direction of C. R. Byrom, Chief Operating Manager, was a stroke of imaginative genius. With the object of appealing to the sporting and competitive instincts of the men a 'punctuality league' system was instituted. It was divided into two parts, covering the local trains, in the fifty-one local operating divisions in England and Wales, and a main line competition between the Western, Midland, Central and Northern Divisions. The local operating divisions were grouped into three leagues, on the basis of their past records in punctuality and at the end of the first year the leaders in one league moved upwards, and the laggards in another moved downwards, as in the football league competitions. This introduction of a sporting aspect to the daily work led to increased keenness, while the whole operation was monitored month by month in the new journal of the Operating Department entitled, *On Time*. Thumbnail biographies of men and women in the department, from the lowest to the highest grades were regularly featured; various aspects of operation were described in fully authoritative feature articles, paying particular attention to individual men and women involved. It was a time when I was becoming increasingly

National Railway Museum

31. The northbound 'Devonian', Torquay to Bradford, leaving Bristol, hauled by Jubilee class 4–6–0 no. 5609, 'Gilbert and Ellice Islands', with narrow high-sided tender.

in touch with the advertising and publicity department at Euston, and it was a pleasure to send them news items for inclusion in *On Time*.

Publicity was given to good runs, with appropriate praise bestowed upon the train crews concerned, and there is no doubt that the spirit engendered by this activity spurred engine crews to make up lost time when they could. Naturally, however, there was a small hard core of cynics who refused to be inspired by the mounting tide of enterprise, and of one of these an amusing tale is to be told. It is about a driver, who we shall call Bill, who positively refused to try and recover lost time whatever the circumstances. One day with a Royal Scot class engine he was working an up express and surprised his guard, who knew him and his habits well, by recovering 8 minutes of a late start between Crewe and Euston. On arrival the guard went up to the engine and remarked: 'You're not running up to form today Bill.' To which Bill replied: 'Wotcher mean: fourteen late off Crewe, fourteen late 'ere!' But unfortunately for Bill he had relied too implicitly upon his young fireman for the point-to-point times, and that young enthusiast had 'accidentally' told him the wrong schedule! Poor Bill: that lapse took some living down at Camden shed!

Byrom's drive for punctuality was not confined to normal times. He impressed upon his staff that at busy week-ends, especially at those of the statutory Bank Holidays, more people would be travelling, and that it was important to impress these casual passengers with the efficiency of railway working. Hitherto, at such times, unpunctuality had been so general and so often considered quite unavoidable, that special reference to the successful working of a difficult group of trains merits special mention, as representing an outcome of

T. G. Hepburn, Rail Archive Stephenson

32. The up 'Merseyside Express' near Brinklow, hauled by the turbine-driven 4–6–2 no. 6202.

the 'on time' drive. In 1934 what was termed the 'six o'clock group' of departures from Euston consisted of the following:

5.50 pm Birmingham and Wolverhampton
6.00 pm 'The Lancastrian' – Manchester
6.05 pm 'The Merseyside Express'
6.10 pm 'The Ulster Express' – Heysham Harbour

In earlier years, with all except the first needing to be run in duplicate on the Friday before a Bank Holiday, they were dispatched at about 3-minute intervals, and the small headways made delays inevitable. Deliberately easy running to avoid checks resulted in the fourth or fifth train of the series being anything up to half an hour late before it was 100 miles out of London, as I experienced several times on 'The Ulster Express'.

Beginning in 1934, however, the second parts of the 6.05 and 6.10 pm expresses were dispatched at 6.15 and 6.20 pm respectively, thus leaving the first parts in their normal paths, with their normal coach formations. A relief of 'The Lancastrian' was run at 5.55 pm so that there was a regular interval of 5 minutes between

Author

33. On the Callander and Oban line: the morning express from Glasgow to Oban, with Pullman observation car 'Maid of Morven' in rear, approaching Crianlarich. The engine is ex-Highland 4–6–0 no. 14768, 'Clan MacKenzie'.

seven successive trains, all of which were non-stop to Crewe or beyond. The result of this careful planning, aided by keen work on the part of the engine crews was almost exact timekeeping at each holiday season. I travelled twice by 'The Merseyside Express' in these conditions, each time worked by a Royal Scot, with a load of 505 tons, and we reached Liverpool exactly on time. What, perhaps, was more remarkable was that this train – and necessarily the other just ahead of it – got an absolutely clear road through such busy centres as Rugby, Stafford and Crewe. It was rather surprising, however, to find a journal of the standing of the *Railway Gazette* rather cynical towards the 'On Time' campaign of the LMS. I sent notes of these Whitsun holiday experiences of mine to them. They were published as editorial notes, with a backhanded epilogue that read: 'The foregoing notes, it is to be confessed, owe their inspiration partly to the joy with which the sinner that repenteth is welcomed, but we must not forget those who have been perhaps less reprehensible in the past . . .', and the comment went on to instance a somewhat irrelevant case on another railway.

Some months earlier the same journal carried a somewhat faint-hearted editorial under the heading: 'The Two-Edged Sword'. It read: 'The January issue of *On Time*, the journal of the LMSR Operating Department, is made the occasion for a New Year message from Mr C. R. Byrom which is as generous in its

National Railway Museum

34. Kyle of Lochalsh station, with ex-Highland 4–6–0 of the Clan Goods class marshalling up an eastbound fish train.

appraisement of punctuality progress in 1935 as it is inspiring in its exhortations for 1936. Mr Byrom shows how widespread is the responsibility for maintaining the "On Time" ideal, and we would add that as the standard is raised, so do the penalties of default and the quarters from which they proceed increase in number. The more fast running is publicised, the greater is the disappointment of travellers at late arrivals. Nor are travellers the only critics. Some accelerated point-to-point runs involve towns where the express service is scanty, and the improvement of facilities has earned initially favourable comment in the local press. The first failure to maintain a record probably hailed as "epoch-making" is eagerly seized upon by inveterate grumblers to write letters claiming that not only has the railway failed to keep its word regarding its premier trains, but is notoriously blind to local requirements in its less spectacular activities. However unjustified, such attacks have a disastrous effect upon railway relationship with the public. Not only is speed a two-edged sword, but the path of acceleration leads to ever widening responsibilities.'

It was astonishing to discern such a timorous

National Railway Museum

35. Jubilee class 4–6–0 no. 5572, 'Irish Free State', at St Pancras having just backed on to its train; the headlamps have not been changed. This engine was renamed 'Eire' in 1938.

attitude towards railway progress in the mid-1930s, or was it that the editorial department of the *Railway Gazette* just did not believe that the LMS meant real business? My own travelling was not very extensive at that time, and was mostly at weekends; but for the record I went through my log book covering the years 1934 and 1935, and found that on the LMS I travelled 4,305 miles, mostly on the LNW and Caledonian sections, and on no more than five occasions – *in two years!* – were we late on arrival. The worst instance was on a Saturday afternoon in high summer when I had been down to Blisworth, for the ride, to log the sharply timed 4.30 pm Birmingham express; and the up day Aberdeen (due in Euston at 7.30 pm) by which I returned from Blisworth was some 40 minutes late arriving from the north, but regained 1½ minutes on its 63-minute schedule to Euston.

Travelling on the line in 1935 I had my first experiences of the new Stanier 4–6–0s. On Whit Tuesday I was on the up 'Mid-day Scot', and with sixteen on a Royal Scot had one of the 5X 4–6–0s as pilot to Shap summit. The two

F. R. Hebron, Rail Archive Stephenson

36. The up 'Mid-day Scot' passing Thankerton in 1936 hauled by the last of the Princess Royal class of 4–6–2s, no. 6212, 'Duchess of Kent'.

engines made light of it, and we left 6 minutes early. The Scot then ran the 37.7 miles down to Lancaster in exactly 36 minutes start to stop, and did well with this heavy train onwards to Crewe. There the load was reduced to 469 tons tare, and one of the new Jubilees took over, no. 5592, then unnamed. The 5X load for 'Special Limit' timings was 415 tons, and we should have been piloted; but none was available, and we made a characteristically bad start for the low-superheat days of those engines, taking no less than 20¾ minutes to get up to Whitmore, 10.7 miles, and falling to 32 mph on the 1 in 177 of Madeley bank. But there must have been a couple of rare sportsmen on the footplate, because having warmed up they coaxed a splendid run out of the engine, covering the 145.2 miles from Whitmore to South

Hampstead in 146½ minutes. Euston was reached in 171½ minutes against the 165-minute scheduled – by no means a discreditable effort with 54 tons overload.

My first run with a 'Black Five' was also in very heavy conditions of loading, on the up 'Ulster Express' on a Sunday morning, 454 tons tare, 490 tons full, and engine no. 5153. Starting from Lancaster I was surprised that no bank engine was taken up to the junction, and the start was slow in consequence; but although subsequent acceleration was not very brisk we got up to 70 mph at Brock troughs, and would have kept time to Preston but for a signal check at Barton. The engine did particularly well from Warrington to Crewe, covering this 24.1 miles in 28½ minutes start to stop, again with no rear-end assistance from the start up to the Ship Canal bridge. One of the best of my early runs with the new engines was on the 4.30 pm Glasgow and Edinburgh express to Liverpool. A Midland compound had made short work of the 5-coach Edinburgh portion to Symington, whence a Baby Scot maintained the sharp point-to-point timings of that train, with a load made up to 410 tons. Then at Carlisle one of the new 5Xs, no. 5573, came on. This train then had almost the same timing as the up 'Royal Scot' with 107 minutes for the 90.1 miles to Preston stop, against the former train's 108 minutes to pass. In view of some of the unkind things said about the Jubilees in their original low-superheat condition I have set the details of this run out in tabular form. The sectional time-keeping was very close, and passing Carnforth 1½ minutes early there was plenty of time for an 'on time' arrival in Preston, but for the concluding checks. It will be seen from the log that the minimum speed on the long 1 in 125 from Clifton to Shap was 28¼ mph and that a maximum of 82 mph was attained before Tebay.

LMS: 7.2 pm CARLISLE–PRESTON
Load: 12 cars, 383 tons tare 410 tons full
Engine: 3 cyl. 4–6–0 no. 5573 (Class 5X)

Dist Miles		Sch min	Actual m s	Speeds mph
0.0	CARLISLE	0	0 00	—
4.9	Wreay		9 55	36
7.4	Southwaite		13 40	46
10.8	Calthwaite		18 17	43
13.1	Plumpton	21	21 22	54/48
17.9	PENRITH	27	26 50	55
20.1	*Milepost 49*		29 13	57½
22.1	Clifton		31 32	45
26.1	*Milepost 43*		38 27	28¼
29.4	Shap		44 53	38
31.4	*Shap summit*	48	48 25	32
37.0	Tebay	54	53 35	82
43.1	Grayrigg		58 57	61
50.0	OXENHOLME	66	65 18	71/65
55.5	Milnthorpe		70 05	73
59.6	*Milepost 9½*		73 42	62
62.8	CARNFORTH	78	76 25	77
66.0	Hest Bank		79 07	72
—			sigs	5
69.1	LANCASTER	84	85 04	
			sigs	30
73.5	Galgate		90 55	53
80.6	Garstang	96	98 13	66
85.4	Barton		*104 05*	sig
—			107 25	stop
88.8	*Oxheys Box*	104	114 37	
			prolonged sigs	
90.1	PRESTON	107	122 25	

Net time 103 minutes
Delays from Lancaster due to Bank Holiday traffic

Before concluding this chapter, and its references to *On Time* I must pass on an amusing experience concerning one of my own photographs that they reproduced. I was lucky enough to catch the morning express from Glasgow to Oban in a highly photogenic setting near Crianlarich, and sent them a copy. The main road in the foreground of the picture was deserted at the time, but the enterprising photographic editor decided to heighten the atmosphere of the scene by skilfully implanting an LMS road motor lorry. The picture eventually appeared above the following stirring caption: 'Far from the busy main line and traffic-jammed city street, by train and motor the banner of "On Time" service is carried into Highland fastnesses.' Silence for a few days, and then, from Glasgow, all hell was let loose. The operating people had instantly recognised that the lorry was not one of a type used anywhere in Scotland, and jumping to the justifiable conclusion that it was a fraudulent trader using the LMS initials illicitly were on the point of taking the matter up with the licensing authorities, when someone thought to ask *On Time* exactly when the photograph was taken. Panic was momentarily transferred to Euston House, until the enterprising photographic editor 'came clean', and admitted that the lorry was 'scooped' from a photograph taken in West Cumberland! For those who may like to look it up the unadulterated photograph appeared as a full page plate in the *Railway Magazine* for January 1937. The last coach of the eight-coach train was the celebrated 'Maid of Morven' observation car in traditional Pullman livery; but in the reproduction in *On Time* this vehicle had been discreetly repainted in Midland red!

7
General Acceleration

It was not to be expected that the faint-hearted attitude of the *Railway Gazette* towards acceleration would give Sir Josiah Stamp and his colleagues any cause to hesitate, or deviate from their chosen programme; and indeed some of the developments in 1936 might have been regarded as venturesome, had the foundations been less solidly laid. The friendly rivalry between the East Coast and West Coast routes to the north had been no more than mildly stirred in the autumn of 1935, when the LNER put on 'The Silver Jubilee' express – Britain's first high speed streamlined train; and although there were frequent disclaimers from Euston House, both private and public, that the LMS were not intending to introduce any trains of that kind, there is no doubt that its great success caused second thoughts in many minds. In the meantime the 'heavy-load' trials of the reboilered Pacific engine, 'The Princess Royal', formed the basis of some notable service improvements on the West Coast main line. There was no question of lightening the loads to permit acceleration. Such was the confidence engendered in the 6203–6212 series of Pacifics that accelerated timings were planned for the heaviest trains. In referring to these engines, however, official sources were, I discovered, rather sensitive towards the phraseology to be used. The description 'Pacific' was barred in case they became confused with the Pacifics of the LNER. In all official correspondence and publicity handouts they were referred to as 4–6–2s.

By the autumn of 1935 it was evident that the ten new engines, together with the reboilered 6200 were doing magnificent work. My own personal experiences of them were at first almost entirely on the Liverpool trains, though on the through workings between Euston and Glasgow a high degree of utilisation was being obtained, with greatly reduced turn-round times at each end. The engines that worked the down 'Night Scot', for example, arriving in Glasgow at 9.35 am returned south on the up 'Mid-day Scot' after no more than 4 hours interval. Without wishing to adopt a partisan attitude I must admit that some of the work I recorded personally on the Liverpool trains in the winter of 1935–6, was superior to anything I had recorded elsewhere in Great Britain up to that time. It seemed that the Princess Royal class engines, with their high-superheat boilers, had definitely got the edge on their famous progenitors on the GWR, much as I have always admired these latter. While the Royal Scots, expertly driven and fired, had been doing splendid work on these trains, the 'Lizzie's', as we came to know them affectionately, seemed to have a vast amount in reserve.

With the down 'Merseyside Express' with the

Author's Collection

37. A dynamometer car test on the Midland Line with one of the later 'Black Fives' with domed boiler, no. 5278 with the Horwich dynamometer car.

usual 15-coach train of 505 tons gross behind the tender, engine no. 6212, 'Duchess of Kent', was 3¾ minutes early by Bletchley, 7½ minutes early at Rugby, and still 5 minutes early at Stafford, after checks on the Trent Valley line. The passing times had been 36 minutes 21 seconds at Tring; 48 minutes 20 seconds at Bletchley; 59 minutes 34 seconds at Roade, and 81 minutes 30 seconds at Rugby. Continuing, Crewe, 158.1 miles, was passed in 161 minutes exactly, and the 189.6 miles to Mossley Hill stop completed in 196 minutes 2 seconds. A few days later I came up on the 6.12 pm up 'Liverpool Flyer' from Crewe, with engine no. 6208, 'Princess Helena Victoria', with a 470-ton load. Before the introduction of the Pacifics – sorry Euston House, 4–6–2s! – this train, subject to the XL limits of loading, was required to be piloted if a Royal Scot had more than 380 tons, and this was almost invariably necessary on Friday nights throughout the year. The Pacific load for this schedule was 420 tons, but such was the confidence drivers gained in these engines that they took loads up to 482 tons tare, without assistance. This was a remarkable revival of the old spirit of the LNWR in which drivers would never hesitate to take 20 or 30 tons over their stipulated loads, and gain time, too.

Hard and successful running on the 'Liverpool Flyer' with heavier than the scheduled loads was by no means the prerogative of the new engines. One evening in July 1933 a Royal Scot was not available, and with a load of 351 tons the Claughton put on in substitution had to be piloted. The assistance, however, a new 6 ft 9 ins, standard class 2 4–4–0, was of no great value and just south of Rugby it failed altogether and had to be detached. The Claughton had 51 tons over the XL limit for a class 5 engine, but her driver went for it in tremendous style, and covered the 74.8 miles from the restart at Hillmorton box to Willesden Junction in 65¾ minutes start to stop, an average of 68.2 mph regaining 2½ minutes on

LMS: 6.12 pm CREWE–WILLESDEN
Running between Welton and Kings Langley
54.4 miles

Engine No.	6130	5967	6200	6207
Engine Name	'Liverpool'	'L/Corpl. J. A. Christie V.C.'	'The Princess Royal'	'Princess Arthur of Connaught'
Load, tons gross	315	370	500	515
Wt. of engine tons	85	77	104½	104½
Nom. T.E. tons	14.8	10.7	18.0	18.0
Time m. s.	43 18	44 48	42 39	46 36
Av. Speed mph	75.3	72.8	76.3	70.0
Ratio: load*: engine	4.34	5.32	5.31	5.32
load*: T.E.	24.9	38.2	30.8	31.6

*Including tender with train

this fast schedule, from Roade. I have not seen any details of a run with a Royal Scot when an overload was taken, but details of this run alongside two very fine Pacific efforts make an interesting comparison having regard to the weight and nominal tractive efforts of the engines concerned. I have taken the comparison only to Kings Langley, because one of the Pacifics was stopped dead by signal just south of that point.

In the above comparison engine no. 6207 was keeping exact schedule time; the others were gaining. The Royal Scot no. 6130 was well within its stipulated load; the Claughton had a 17 per cent excess, and the two Pacifics, 10.95 and 14.8 per cent excess – all on the tare weight of the coaches. In the matter of load to tractive effort the Claughton had considerably the hardest task and her crew deserve every congratulation for so sporting an effort. Unfortunately, at the time it escaped the limelight of *On Time*, and did not come to my own notice until more than thirty years after it had occurred.

In the summer of 1936 there came the notable acceleration of the 'Mid-day Scot'. The dynamometer car test run with engine no. 6200, in May 1935, referred to briefly in Chapter 4, paved the way for this development. The test train was stopped at Lancaster, and then made a remarkable climb to Shap, passing the summit 37.7 miles from the restart in 41¾ minutes, with a load of 465 tons. The 'Mid-day Scot' had previously run non-stop between Lancaster and Carlisle, but this demonstration of locomotive capacity tempted the operating department to insert a stop at Penrith, to facilitate tourist traffic to the Lake District, within the accelerated schedule of 7 hours 35 minutes from Euston to Glasgow. Moreover, the full load was carried through to Carlisle; and with the addition of the Plymouth coaches at Crewe the minimum formation was fourteen coaches, with a tare load of about 445 tons. Against the test result of 41¾ minutes from Lancaster to Shap summit the service train was given 45 minutes and another 14 minutes, for the subsequent 13.5 mile downhill run to the stop at Penrith. It proved a very severe assignment, all the more so as coming in the course of a 400-mile through locomotive working. The engine crews concerned, from Crewe North and Polmadie sheds

THE MID-DAY SCOT – 1936
LANCASTER–PENRITH IN 59 MINUTES

Engine 4–6–2 no.			6203	6205	6208	6209	6206	6208	6212	6210
Load, tons gross trailing			470	470	470	470	475	515	520	530
Dist		Sch	Actual	Actual	Actual	Actual	Actual	Actual	Actual	Actual
Miles		m	m s	m s	m s	m s	m s	m s	m s	m s
0.0	LANCASTER	0	0 00	0 00	0 00	0 00	0 00	0 00	0 00	0 00
6.3	CARNFORTH	8	8 01	8 00	8 20	7 39	8 28	7 52	8 40	8 34
19.1	Oxenholme	21	20 44	21 53	22 52	19 50	22 41	20 25	22 23	22 28
26.2	Grayrigg	—	30 21	31 21	33 00	29 02	33 33	29 21	32 06	32 06
32.2	Tebay	36	36 31	37 45	39 23	34 48	39 53	35 15	38 09	38 20
37.7	Shap summit	45	44 19	46 29	48 34	43 10	48 21	43 30	46 30	47 16
51.2	PENRITH	59	57 34	59 31	62 16	56 24	60 24	56 10	59 26	60 07
Av. Speed		mph								
Carnforth–Summit			51.8	48.9	46.8	53.1	47.3	52.8	49.8	48.7
Max speed		mph	67	64½	64	70½	64	71	64	63
Min speed		mph	31½	30	23½	27½	26	28½	27½	29
Average approx. Equivalent dhp			1510	1410	1320	1570	1370	1690	1570	1550

on alternate days would, it is true, have begun their duty only 80 minutes earlier; but the locomotive itself would have been on the road for 230 miles.

In the first weeks of its operation there were eight detailed records of the running between Lancaster and Penrith, and these eight runs featured seven different engines of the 6203–6212 series of Pacifics. The details, which are important as representing what was probably the hardest daily task yet set to British locomotives by that time, suggest that it was the personalities and individual skills of the engine crews rather than locomotive capacity that governed the success, or otherwise of the performance, and in the adjoining table it will be seen that the slowest and the fastest run were made by the same engine, the latter with two additional coaches. In the table I have shown the average speeds maintained in climbing the 31.4 miles from Carnforth to Shap summit, a vertical rise of 885 ft, and an estimate of the equivalent horsepower sustained at the tender drawbar, making allowance for the initial and final speeds. It will be seen that the average horsepower varied between 1,320 and 1,685, while it will be realised that the maximum figures would be higher than this. The climb from Carnforth to Shap summit includes two stretches of easier grading where drivers would obviously take the opportunity of steaming their engines lightly, if only for a short time.

At times of maximum loading the up 'Mid-day Scot' was another severe assignment, because from Carlisle southwards it carried through carriages from Stranraer – providing the daytime service from Belfast to Euston. I travelled by the train throughout from Glasgow in May 1937, and the tare loads were 310 tons from the start, 478 tons from Symington, and

M. W. Earley

38. The 'Royal Scot' climbing Shap: a fifteen-car train hauled by 4–6–2 no. 6207, 'Princess Arthur of Connaught'.

no less than 532 tons (eighteen vehicles) from Carlisle. The working was punctual throughout, with engine no. 6206, 'Princess Marie Louise'. In this direction the train was allowed 81 minutes start to stop for the 69.1 miles from Carlisle to Lancaster, and with a gross trailing load of 570 tons the 31.4 miles up to Shap summit, from a standing start took 42½ minutes, passing the summit 1½ minutes early. On the long 1 in 125 gradient from Clifton speed was sustained at 41 mph requiring an output of 1,805 equivalent drawbar horsepower. The last stage of this 400-mile working, still with a load of 570 tons, involved running the 158 miles from Crewe to Euston non-stop in 164 minutes (57.8 mph) which task was accomplished with 40 seconds to spare.

While from the autumn of 1935 the performances of the Princess Royal class engine formed the 'neon-lights' display of the locomotive department, the taper-boilered 5Xs were gradually coming into their own. The LMS certainly took a rise out of the Great Western on the competitive London–Birmingham service, for while the latter company felt the need to *decelerate* some of the trains

40. Somerset and Dorset Line: the northbound 'Pines Express' passing Wellow, hauled by ex-Midland 7 ft rebuilt 4–4–0 no. 518 and a standard 2P 4–4–0 no. 630.

National Railway Museum

39. 'The Permanent Way – Relaying', a popular example of an LMS poster.

L & GRP, Courtesy David and Charles

F. R. Hebron, Rail Archive Stephenson

41. A train of coal empties passing Elstree, and stretching out of sight round the far curve in the photograph. The engine is 2–6–0 + 0–6–2 Beyer-Garratt no. 4994.

previously booked to an overall time of 2 hours, the LMS clipped 5 minutes from some of those making only one intermediate stop. On these trains, the low-superheat Jubilees were rather slow in getting off the mark, but ran well enough afterwards. On the 11.30 am down from Euston, with a 9-car train, no. 5597, 'Barbados', took 11½ minutes to pass Willesden Junction, and was then doing only 53 mph; but then she went on to cover the 62.8 miles from Watford to Hillmorton at an average speed of 70 mph, and completed the 94 miles to Coventry stop in 91¾ minutes. With a good finish Birmingham was reached in exactly 5 minutes under the 2 hours.

Inevitably LMS running came under some comparison with the Silver Jubilee of the LNER but never more amusingly than one night when the up 'Liverpool Flyer' was loaded to 391 tons, and had a high-superheat Jubilee as train engine. From Liverpool the pilot had been a George the Fifth class 4–4–0, but ever since one of them, in a very run down condition, nearly rattled its cab off on the fast run to Willesden, they were not permitted on this train south of Crewe, and on this occasion a Baby Scot was coupled on instead. This meant the two 5Xs, one of each kind, had a load of 415 tons between them. Never previously on the LMS had I logged such a riot of a run as followed. It was a time of heavy traffic, and three times on the way up we were pulled up dead by signals, in addition to experiencing two other checks; but despite all this hindrance we covered the 152.7 miles from Crewe to Willesden in 140½ minutes start to

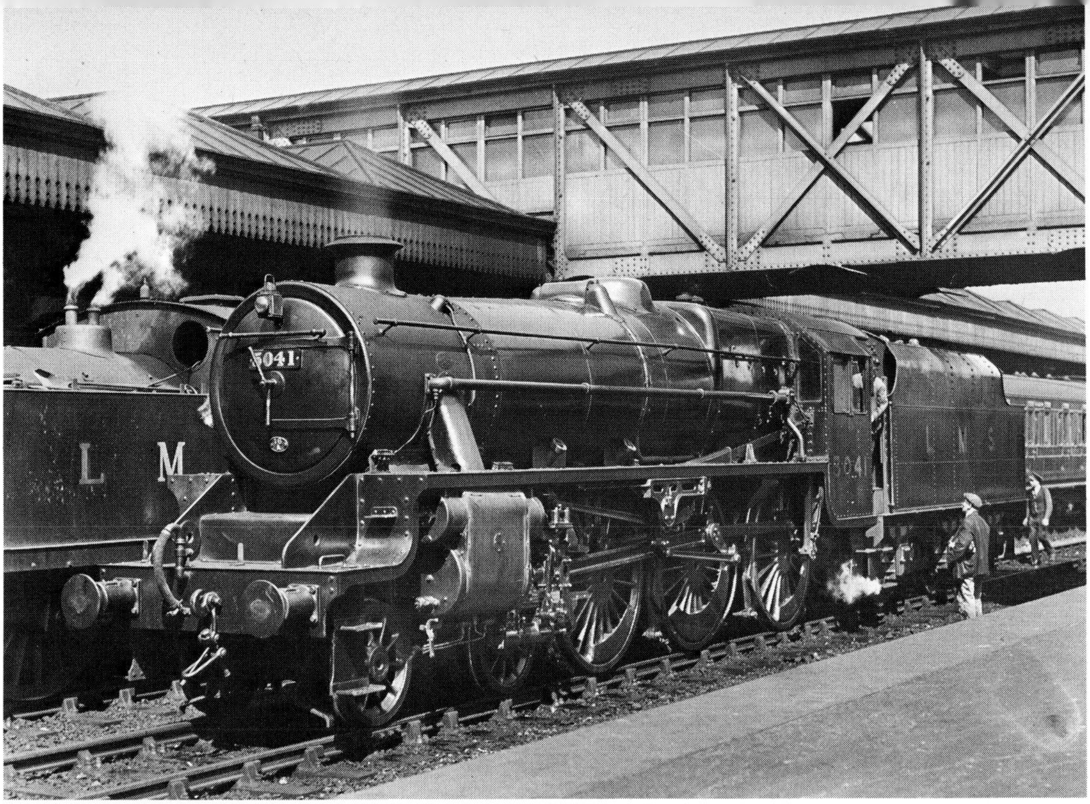

T. G. Hepburn, Rail Archive Stephenson

42. A fine impression of one of those excellent workhorses for all duties, a standard 'Black Five' 4–6–0 no. 5041 at Nottingham.

stop, arriving 1½ minutes, inside schedule time. Between them the five checks cost 15 minutes in running, which left a net time of 125½ minutes, an average of exactly 73 mph. An aggregate of no less than 99 miles of the journey were run at 80 mph. Maximum speeds of around 85 mph were too numerous to mention individually, but we reached 88 mph twice, before Rugby and before Weedon, and a full 90 was attained twice, before Castlethorpe and in a final dash through Kenton. As a friend remarked at the time, this was running up to LNER Silver Jubilee standard, but with 5X 4–6–0s instead of an A4 Pacific. The load to each engine was 207 tons, against 230. For the record the LMS engines were no. 5524, 'Sir Frederick Harrison', leading, and no. 5673, then unnamed.

There was an amusing sequel to this run. A brief note of it was published in the *Railway Gazette*, and caused something of a stir in LMS circles. The Chief Civil Engineer immediately rang up the Operating Department and accused them of grossly exceeding the speed limits, averring that such a time could not possibly have been made without serious excess at Stafford and Rugby. As it was a case of a press release reference was made to the publicity people, who had my log. It was then quietly pointed out that far from exceeding speed limits the train had been stopped by signal at both Stafford and Rugby!

8
1937: A Great Year for the LMS

The great centralising, national and imperial occasion of a memorable year, the coronation of their Majesties King George VI and Queen Elizabeth, on 12 May, was equally the focus point of many special railway activities; but for the LMS another great occasion had long previously been foreshadowed, namely the Centenary of Euston. Even then, however, its complete reconstruction was foreshadowed and in the opening sentences of a notable anniversary article in the *Railway Magazine* D. S. Barrie wrote: 'Yet for all the modernity of the great system of which it is the headquarters, Euston is essentially old fashioned; the long platforms, the great Doric arch that knew the fulsome flattery of Victorian essayists, today withstand with equal composure the assaults of Georgian journalists. It is in keeping with that strict sense of propriety with which Euston has always aloofly confronted the pinpricks of progress that it should survive in its present form to celebrate its centenary, before making way for the newer and greater Euston that is to come. For on its hundredth birthday Euston faces as complete, as thorough, and (as some people would no doubt like to phrase it) as salutary and as wholesome a reconstruction as could possibly happen to it. The old buildings, the rambling platforms, and the scattered facilities that form the dubious legacy of a century of piecemeal enlargement are to disappear, and a newer and finer model station is to emerge from the ruins.'

Had it been possible for the aspirations and plans of Sir Josiah Stamp, and his Board, to be put promptly into effect it is more than likely that the demolition of the Doric Arch, and the Great Hall would, in the spirit of that age, have passed with no more than a few discordant comments. The railway preservation movement had scarcely begun, and publicity was constantly directed towards what was new, than to any sense of appreciation of what had been done in the past. It was essential to build up a towering image of the new, vital, modern railway, rather than recall the heritage it had in the achievements of the constituent companies. It was all part of the continuing need to erase memories of the bad early days of the amalgamation, when factional in-fighting did so much harm. As things turned out it was not until 14 October 1968 that Her Majesty Queen Elizabeth II opened the rebuilt Euston; and although it proved to be an admirable layout from the purely utilitarian business of handling

BBC Hulton Picture Library

43. Prelude to the 'Coronation Scot': the crowd surrounding engine no. 6201, 'Princess Elizabeth', at Euston on 17 November 1936. She has run the 401½ miles from Glasgow non-stop in 5 hours 44¼ minutes.

the traffic the appearance, particularly as seen from Euston Road, is quite undistinguished compared with what was proposed in the scheme first envisaged in the 1930s.

From an artist's impression reproduced in the *Railway Magazine* of October 1968, it is clear that use of the Doric Arch did not enter into the new proposals. At the time, however, the plan of reconstruction, as represented in this drawing, was not generally known and there was considerable discussion as to what should be done with the Arch. One proposal was to move it to form the centre piece of the new entrance from Euston Road. Such a procedure would not necessarily have meant dismantling and rebuilding it in the new position, and attention was drawn to a remarkable feat in Hartford, Connecticut, USA, in which a 9-storey building weighing 8,000 tons, had been *rolled* to a new site 112 ft from its original position. The building was of the steel frame and brick curtain-wall type. The actual moving took two days, and during this time, and the preparations for moving, business went on as usual in the building; the lifts continued to function, and water,

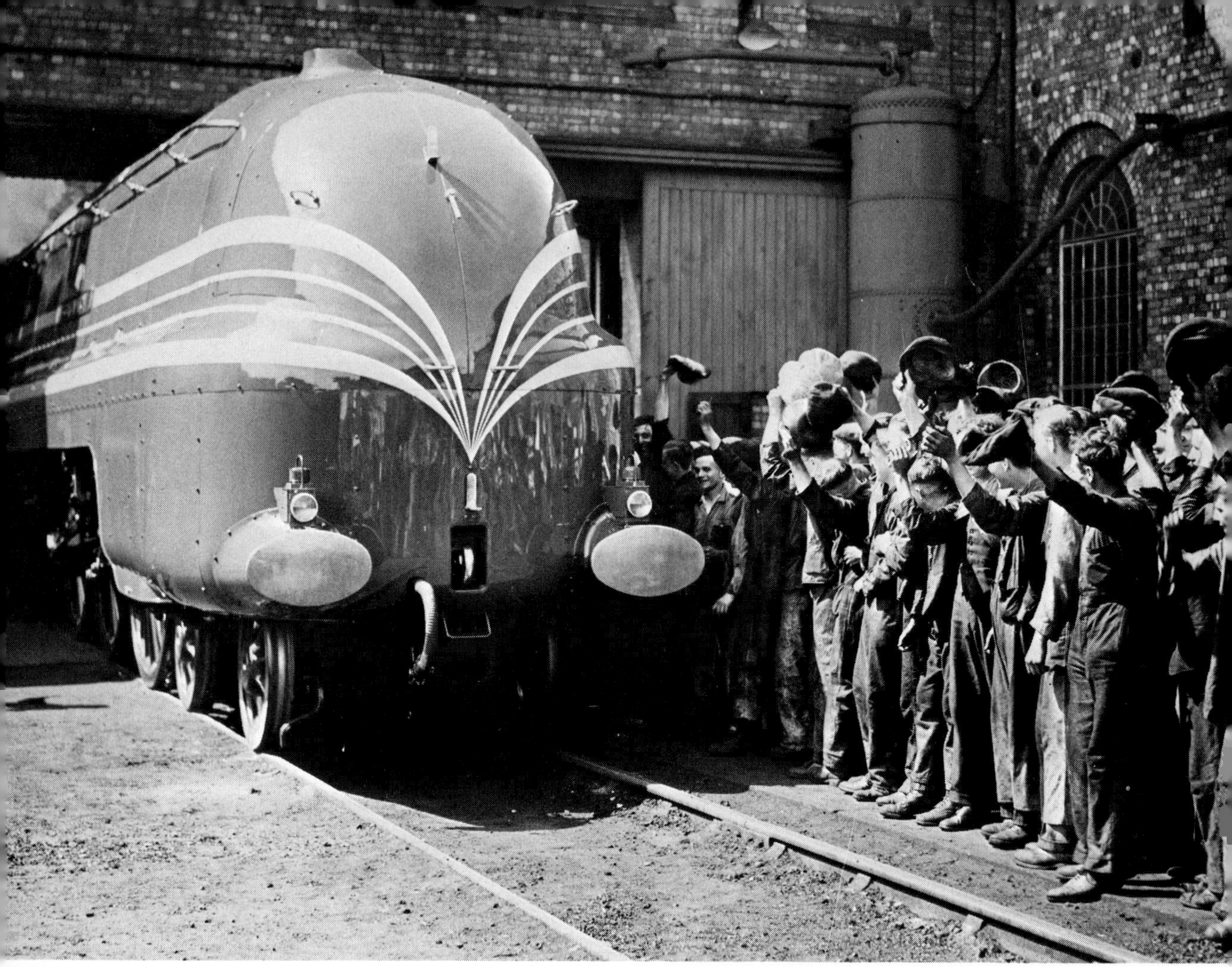

Author's Collection

44. The first of the streamliners, no. 6220, 'Coronation', making a ceremonial emergence from the erecting shop at Crewe.

drainage, gas and electric services were maintained. Fascinating though the prospect might have been for rolling the Doric Arch one must admit that it would have looked somewhat out of place in front of the planned building.

The approach to Coronation year in 1937 brought some revised thinking so far as the West Coast main line passenger services were concerned. The accelerated services between Euston and Glasgow operated during the summer of 1936 maintained relative equality with those of the East Coast route from King's Cross to Edinburgh, both operated on occasions with very heavy trains. When, however, it became known that the LNER were proposing to put on a new high-speed streamlined train, in the style and speed of the 'Silver

Author's Collection

45. It gives a strange effect when the access doors of a streamliner are opened to get to the smokebox door.

Jubilee', cutting the overall time from King's Cross to Edinburgh from the 7½ hours of the summer non-stop 'Flying Scotsman' to the level *6 hours*, it was felt that the LMS could no longer stand aloof, as it were, from the light-weight, high-speed, streamline business. Their supporters hoped that a 6-hour service from Euston to Glasgow would be introduced. With a strictly limited load, like that of the 'Silver Jubilee', it seemed eminently practicable with the fine modern locomotives; and confirmation of this was not long in coming when the celebrated non-stop runs between Euston and Glasgow were made on 16 and 17 November 1936 with engine no. 6201, 'Princess Elizabeth', hauling seven cars northbound, and eight cars on the return. The overall times were 5 hours 53½ minutes and 5 hours 44¼ minutes respectively. The fact that these spectacular runs were prefaced, both in London and Glasgow, by circumstances that might have dissuaded any

Author's Collection

46. Three streamliners alongside at Crewe: 'Queen Mary', 'Queen Elizabeth' and 'Coronation'.

less resolute a personality than R. A. Riddles from making the runs at all were not generally known at the time. But I have told this side of the story elsewhere. So far as the present theme is concerned the runs were triumphantly made, in rough wintry weather, and the stage seemed set for a 6-hour London–Glasgow service.

The technical details of those runs, as carefully recorded in the dynamometer car, and observed by Riddles himself from the footplate suggested that in a locomotive intended for continuous high-speed running certain modifications to the Princess Royal design could advantageously be made, notably by an improved layout of steam and exhaust passages incorporating a degree of internal streamlining, and a still higher degree of superheat in the boiler. It is of interest to recall that at the time of making those very fast non-stop runs to and from Glasgow engine no. 6201 had a boiler that was different from all other engines of the class. While no. 6200 had a new boiler with a reduced distance between the tube plates no. 6201 retained the original boiler, but modified to have a 32-element superheater and enlarged tubes. In view of the historic importance of her runs the three stages of boiler development on the Princess Royal class are set down in tabular form:

Boilers: Princess Royal class 4–6–2s

Engines	6200 6201 original	6200 6203–12	6201 modified
Tubes			
small, number	170	112	119
outside dia. ins	$2\frac{1}{4}$	$2\frac{3}{8}$	$2\frac{3}{8}$
large, number	16	32	32
outside dia. ins	$5\frac{1}{8}$	$5\frac{1}{8}$	$5\frac{1}{8}$
Length between tube plates ft ins	20–9	19–3	20–9
Heating surfaces sq. ft			
tubes	2523	2299	2429
firebox	190	217	190
superheater	370	598	594
total	3083	3114	3213

The modified boiler on no. 6201 also had a dome set on the most rearward ring.

National Railway Museum

47. Right away! The 'Coronation Scot' hauled by 4–6–2 no. 6222, 'Queen Mary', at the moment of starting from no. 13 platform at Euston in July 1937.

By the autumn of 1936 Stanier, by the build-up of his organisation, his outstanding ability as a 'works' man and no less by his charming and equable personality, had already attained a positively towering status in the railway world; and when in that same autumn the Government of India, alarmed at the worsening financial condition of the State-owned railways decided that an expert inquiry should be set up, Stanier, together with Sir Ralph Wedgwood, Chief General Manager of the LNER were invited to form the two-men Committee of Inquiry. And so, in November 1936, just when preparations for the new high-speed service for Coronation year were getting under way, Stanier left for India. In his absence overall responsibility for the CME's department of the LMS was vested in S. J. Symes, the Chief Stores Superintendent, but responsibility for the detailed design and construction of the new Pacific locomotives was in the hands of R. A. Riddles, as Principal Assistant to the CME, and T. F. Coleman, the Chief Draughtsman.

At the risk of stirring the shades of Sir Nigel Gresley I think it can be said that the Princess-Coronation class of Pacifics, as they were officially known at first, represented the most advanced design of express passenger steam locomotive that was ever produced in Great Britain. Apart from the external streamlining, which was afterwards removed, as not being worth the extra weight and the inconvenience it caused in maintenance, the principal outward change was the use of only two sets of valve gear (the valves for the inside cylinders being driven by rocking shafts from the outside gear) and use of a much larger boiler, and firebox. The total heating surface was increased from 2,967 to 3,637 sq. ft; the superheater had forty instead of thirty-two elements, increasing the heating surface from 653 to 830 sq. ft, and the grate area was increased from 45 to 50 sq. ft. Yet such were the advanced features of design incorporated that the total weight of the non-streamlined version of these engines came out at no more than ¾ ton heavier than the Princess Royals.

The tenders were fitted with steam operated coal pushers, which were a great boon to the firemen on a long run. Quite apart from this, from my own experience on the footplate, those large grates were without question the easiest to fire that I have ever observed on a big locomotive. In the course of time I was privileged to have many opportunities of seeing, at first hand, the working of these engines, and there was none of the need for accurate and arduous placing of the coal that was needed on some other designs one could name. The coal was gently fed through the door and it appeared to distribute itself ideally over the grate. At the same time I must add that although very free steaming the engines were very thirsty things; and anywhere away from the old LNWR main line with its liberal provision of water troughs an engine crew had to be very careful of their water supply. Although it is carrying the story long beyond LMS days this slight weakness caused a little embarrassment when one of these engines ran dynamometer car trials on the 'Cornish Riviera Express' in 1956. Taken all round, however, Stanier's men produced a brilliantly successful engine for Coronation year. The form of the streamlining on the original engines of the class, as compared with that on the LNER A4s, was a matter of hot debate among youthful enthusiasts; but really it did not make a great deal of difference, except for being good for publicity!

There was much disappointment among supporters of the LMS when it was announced that the 'Coronation Scot' express would not, after all, make the anticipated 6-hour run between Euston and Glasgow, but would take 6½ hours, with an intermediate stop at Carlisle. From the practical point of view, however, there was every justification for starting this new high-speed service with plenty in hand, and maintaining strict punctuality in all conditions of weather, rather than pitching the standards of working ace-high from the very start. But before the new service began a rousing demonstration of what the new engines could do was given on the Invitation Run for the Press and distinguished guests from Euston to Crewe and back on 29 June 1937. Much has been written of the hair-raising climax to the down journey, when a maximum speed of 114 mph was reached by prolonging the effort down the Madeley bank a little too near to Crewe for comfort; but the return run on which the 158.1 miles to Euston were covered in 119 minutes start to stop was a splendid demonstration of locomotive capacity. In regular service, however, with a train having a tare weight of no more than 297 tons, a timing of 283 minutes for the 299.1 miles between Euston and Carlisle did not impose a very severe burden on locomotives of such quality. A point of significance was that with a departure time of 1.30 pm from each

E. R. Wethersett, Author's Collection

48. The 'Coronation Scot' climbing Camden bank: a fine shot showing the burrowing junctions used for empty stock and engine movements. The streamlined engine is no. 6221, 'Queen Elizabeth'.

terminus the Coronation Scot largely displaced the Midday Scot as the crack afternoon Anglo–Scottish service, and the most exacting 59 minutes booking from Lancaster to Penrith referred to in the previous chapter disappeared.

The seal was finally set upon the success of the Stanier regime in the locomotive department by the dynamometer car test runs conducted in October 1937 with the 5X class 4–6–0 engine no. 5660, 'Rooke', between Bristol and Glasgow. These tests, made with a special train having a tare weight of 302 tons, had the object of establishing the basis for accelerated schedules over the West of England main line, and between Leeds and Glasgow, via the Midland and G&SW route. Extending over four days, some hard running was involved, and although the experimental schedules laid down showed a total cut of 69 minutes below the fastest

Run	Oct. 12 Bristol–Leeds	Oct. 13 Leeds–Glasgow	Oct. 14 Glasgow–Leeds	Oct. 15 Leeds–Bristol
Dist. miles	205.9	228.5	228.5	205.9
Actual time min	223	243½	241¼	223½
Average speed mph	55.4	56.3	56.8	55.3

times then operating over the total distance of 868.8 miles, the actual running times achieved resulted in a further cut of nearly 20 minutes. The four days may be summarised as above.

The foregoing running times included slowing down for and accelerating from intermediate stops at Gloucester, Cheltenham, Birmingham, Derby, Sheffield, Leeds, Carlisle, Annan, Dumfries and Kilmarnock. On the northbound run an additional stop was made at Bromsgrove for banking assistance up the Lickey incline, while southbound, the regulation stop to test brakes was made at the top of the incline, at Blackwell. The merit of the average speeds maintained was emphasised by a complete set of gradient and speed diagrams published in the *Railway Gazette* for 12 November 1937. Based on the results obtained from these trials accelerated schedules were introduced in 1938, though on these double-heading was frequently necessary when 5X class engines were not available.

9
Improving the Line

On any railway, at any time, the activities of the motive power department form a natural focus point of interest, both for enthusiastic onlookers and for professional engineers; but on a line of such intense traffic as that of the LMS the successful development of many other closely allied engineering activities is essential to enable the potentiality of the locomotives to be exploited to the best advantage. First and foremost, of course, there is the track. The London and North Western Railway proudly claimed to have the best permanent way in the world, and in the 1930s the West Coast main line between Euston and Carlisle could certainly be set down as second to none, if not perhaps attaining a position of outright supremacy. Nevertheless, while the LNWR had done much to improve junction layouts, using the 'fly over' to avoid the surface crossing of conflicting routes, there were some awkward alignments that necessitated the retention of permanent speed restrictions at a fairly low level. Of these there was no more hampering a case than Trent Valley Junction, about ½ mile south of Stafford station. The original route, the main line of the Grand Junction southward towards Wolverhampton, had much the better alignment. The Trent Valley line veering away sharply to the east required a speed reduction to 30 mph. The hindrance to fast trains was twofold: the slowing down and regaining of speed involved loss of time; the effect on locomotives was to increase coal consumption.

In 1938 a fairly extensive remodelling of the junction was undertaken. The situation was complicated in that the disposition of the fast and slow lines in the quadruple-tracked routes north and south of Stafford was not the same, and that for convenience in the station working the necessary crossover facilities had been made as part of the general layout at Trent Valley Junction. The principal aim in the remodelling was so to improve the alignment of the down and up main line connections to the Trent Valley section as to permit raising the speed restriction from 30 to 55 mph. Fortunately there was space for considerable slewing of the tracks, to enable the radius of curvature to be reduced, but in addition the actual turnouts, at the junctions were much improved by the use of 'two-level' chairs, and switches longer than the normal British Standard 'D' type. The 'two-level' chair, which had been developed by the Chief Civil Engineer's department of the LMS, and which had first been used at Barassie Junction on the Glasgow–Ayr main line, provides for differential canting, and level, for the diverging road. Another improvement in the revised layout at Trent Valley Junction was the use of movable switch diamonds on the intersection where the down fast line crosses the up line to Birmingham. I made a number of runs

John Edgington

49. Trent Valley junction after remodelling: main line to Rugby to left; old Grand Junction line to Birmingham at right. Note movable diamond crossing of down main and up Grand Junction line.

over the route in the late autumn of 1938, and at speeds of 50 to 55 mph the trains rode the junctions without giving any impression that there was a turnout at all, unlike an occasion back in 1929 when the driver of a Royal Scot ran through Stafford station at 68 mph and took the facing junction at 56 mph. The dining car crew and passengers at dinner were not amused!

In providing for the safe running of the accelerated trains the important relationship between signalling and brake power was carefully developed. This country had already seen the anomalous situation, on another railway, of a very high speed train having to be restricted in maximum speed over the one section of line equipped with modern colour light signalling, because the signal spacing did not provide adequate braking distance for the new train at its maximum. A difficulty that occurred in the operation of steam hauled, high-speed trains was that the weight of the locomotive was high in relation to that of the coaching stock; and since brakes on the bogie and trailing wheels on locomotives had been discarded in the interests of simplicity the locomotive was the most lightly braked vehicle in the train. So, the service braking distance of the 315-ton 'Coronation Scot' running at 80 mph was longer than that of the 520-ton 'Merseyside Express' at the same speed and hauled by the same class of locomotive. Stanier had brought with him from the Great Western the Swindon-designed direct-admission valve, and this was being adopted as standard on the LMS.

With the ordinary vacuum brake air from the driver's brake valve had to flow down the train pipe, and fill the cylinders on every coach to secure a brake application; but with the D.A. valve, as it was known, the admission air passing down the train pipe opened each D.A. valve independently to admit air to the vacuum

Author's Collection

50. Automatic Train Control on the Southend line: close-up of track inductors on a double-slip crossing. The engine is an ex-LTSR 4–4–2 tank.

Reprinted from MODERN TRANSPORT September 17, 1938.

"THE TIMES" OF THE TRANSPORT WORLD.

THE L.M.S. TO-DAY.

Members of the Executive and Some Chief Officers.

SIR WILLIAM V. WOOD,
Vice-President (Finance and Service Departments).

Mr. E. J. H. LEMON, O.B.E.,
Vice-President (Railway Traffic Operating and Commercial). At present in Government Service.

SIR HAROLD HARTLEY, C.B.E., F.R.S.,
Vice-President (Works and Ancillary Undertakings) and Director of Scientific Research.

Mr. ASHTON DAVIES, O.B.E.,
Chief Commercial Manager; Acting Vice-President (Railway Traffic Operating and Commercial Section).

Mr. H. L. THORNHILL,
Chief Legal Adviser.

Mr. O. GLYNNE ROBERTS, O.B.E.,
Secretary.

Mr. H. V. MOSLEY,
Chief Executive Officer for New Works and Parliamentary Business.

Mr. G. L. DARBYSHIRE,
Chief Officer for Labour and Establishment.

Mr. J. BALLANTYNE,
Chief Officer for Scotland.

Mr. W. K. WALLACE,
Chief Civil Engineer.

Mr. T. W. ROYLE, M.B.E.,
Chief Operating Manager.

Mr. T. E. ARGILE,
Acting Chief Commercial Manager.

Mr. GEORGE MORTON,
Chief Accountant.

Mr. W. A. STANIER,
Chief Mechanical Engineer.

Mr. A. F. BOUND,
Signal and Telegraph Engineer.

Photo] [Railway Gazette

Mr. C. E. FAIRBURN,
Deputy Chief Mechanical Engineer and Electrical Engineer.

National Railway Museum

51. Members of the Executive and some Chief Officers.

T. G. Hepburn, Rail Archive Stephenson

52. Standard 8F 2–8–0 no. 8069, forerunner of a very large number of these engines built for general service in Great Britain during the Second World War, and for overseas. The locomotive is climbing out of Nottingham with a Toton–Brent coal train in 1938.

cylinders direct from the atmosphere to a degree directly proportional to the condition of the train pipe. Thus the air for brake application from the driver's valve had only to fill the train pipe and was not required for cylinder application. The train pipe was of very small volume and was rapidly filled with air, and as a consequence the rapidity of operation was not only much increased but was more nearly simultaneous along the length of a train instead of being progressive.

Surprise was sometimes expressed in professional circles that, following the appointment of so hitherto progressive and forward-looking an engineer as A. F. Bound to the high office of Chief Signal and Telegraph Engineer, greater

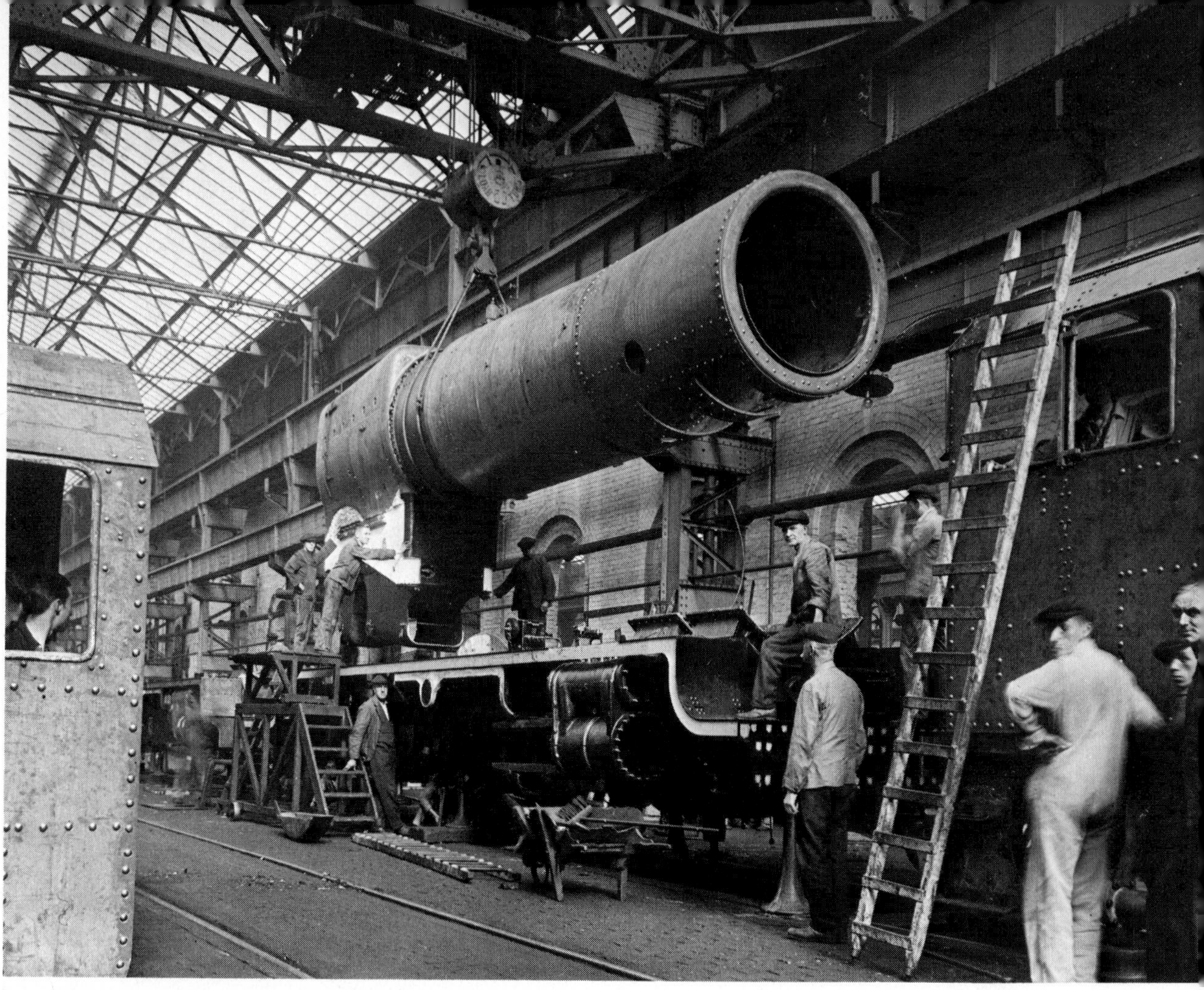

BBC Hulton Picture Library

53. Building the Stanier standard engines at Crewe: lowering the boiler onto the frames.

progress had not been made in modernising the signalling on the line, particularly in view of the notable work currently in progress on the LNER and on the Southern. There is little doubt, however, that Bound's adventure into 'speed signalling' at Mirfield had not been very favourably received, and in the difficult financial circumstances of the mid-1930s funds may not have been available for major resignalling schemes. But important, if less spectacular progress was made towards the operation of the accelerated train service by re-siting distant signals at greater distance from their related stop signals, to give greater braking distance. More significant, however, was that the re-sited distants were almost all of the long range colour light type. On the quadruple-tracked sections, to give uninterrupted long sighting, many of these new signals were carried on gantries spanning all the tracks. There was no change in the ordinary block working, because these colour light distant signals were controlled from circuit breakers fitted to the existing mechanical signal levers.

Another important development, initially on a relatively small scale, was the introduction of automatic train control. While the Great Western Railway had been to the fore in introducing, and bringing to a high degree of perfection a system of audible cab signalling, with control of the train brakes, Bound himself, when Signal Superintendent of the Great Central Railway, had designed and installed a system that provided the same safeguards, initiated by mechanical contact between apparatus on the locomotive and at the line-side. In 1931, however, a demonstration on the West of England main line of the Southern Railway, at Byfleet, of the Strowger-Hudd system, clearly indicated the advantages to be derived from a method of actuation that involved no physical contact between apparatus on the locomotive and on the track; and this demonstration was both important and historic in that it formed the starting point for the present standard automatic warning system on British Railways. It was, however, on the LMS, under Bound's direction, and not on the Southern, that the subsequent development took place.

The basic principles involved, in so far as the indications given to the driver were concerned, were the same as in the well-established Great Western system, on which, incidentally, Stanier himself had read a paper before the Institution of Mechanical Engineers as long ago as 18 December 1914. The system was based upon the indication displayed by each distant signal with distinctively different audible signals in the cab, corresponding to the clear and warning position of the line-side signal. The connecting link, however, was inductive rather than through a contact ramp, as on the GWR. As first used on the LMS it was installed on the former London, Tilbury and Southend line, between Campbell Road Junction, Bow and the terminus at Shoeburyness, a distance of 37 miles. The equipment was installed at 112 distant signal locations, and proving successful formed the basis of the present British Railways standard system. As on the GWR the apparatus included provision for an automatic application on the brakes if a driver did not acknowledge receipt of an audible warning in the cab, if a distant signal in the caution position was being approached.

The year 1937 had witnessed some important organisational changes in the engineering departments. The Board decided to amalgamate the Electrical Department with that of the Chief Mechanical Engineer, thus bringing the LMS into line with the practice of the Great Western and of the LNER in this respect. In consequence of this change C. E. Fairburn, who had held the post of Electrical Engineer of the company since 1934, was appointed to the new office of Deputy Chief Mechanical Engineer, and Electrical Engineer. R. A. Riddles, who from August 1935 had been Principal Assistant to the CME, was appointed Mechanical and Electrical Engineer Scotland. As mentioned earlier in this book the title of his previous office was the same as that Stanier himself held on the GWR where it had the status, virtually, of deputy CME; but it had not been the same on the LMS, and on Riddles's appointment to Scotland, *four* principal assistants to the CME were appointed, sectionalising the duties as follows:

Locomotives	H. G. Ivatt
Carriages and Wagons	J. Purves
Electrical Engineering	F. A. Harper
Outdoor Machinery	J. Boyd

H. G. Ivatt, of course, was a son of H. A. Ivatt the celebrated locomotive engineer of the Great Northern Railway, and himself became Chief Mechanical Engineer of the LMS in January 1946.

T. G. Hepburn, Rail Archive Stephenson

54. 'Black Fives' on the Highland: the 'North Mail' at Dingwall, hauled by no. 5029. The second vehicle is a Highland TPO van, and the third, an ex-LYR dining car.

A notable retirement from high office came in May 1938, when C. R. Byrom, Chief Operating Manager since 1932, handed over to his successor, T. W. Royle. Byrom, as mentioned earlier in this book, was an ex-LNWR man having joined the service as long previously as 1896, and as early as 1918 been promoted to Assistant Superintendent of the Line, under Lancelot W. Horne. He had become Chief General Superintendent of the LMS in 1927, and was appointed to his final post in 1932. He retired in happy circumstances, at the conclusion of his sixty-fourth journey with the Royal Train, in the course of which His Majesty King George VI invested him with the C.V.O. No epoch-making changes followed his retirement. The great organisation for which he had been responsible was in excellent shape, and T. W. Royle took over from 1 June. The new Chief Operating Manager was an ex-LYR man, having joined the service in 1898, and had indeed spent the whole of his career in the north. In view of Byrom's almost contemporary appointment on the LNWR it is interesting to recall that in February 1919 Royle was appointed Assistant Superintendent of the Line, on the Lancashire and Yorkshire Railway.

Some statistics of the operating department of the LMS make interesting reading, as in 1938.

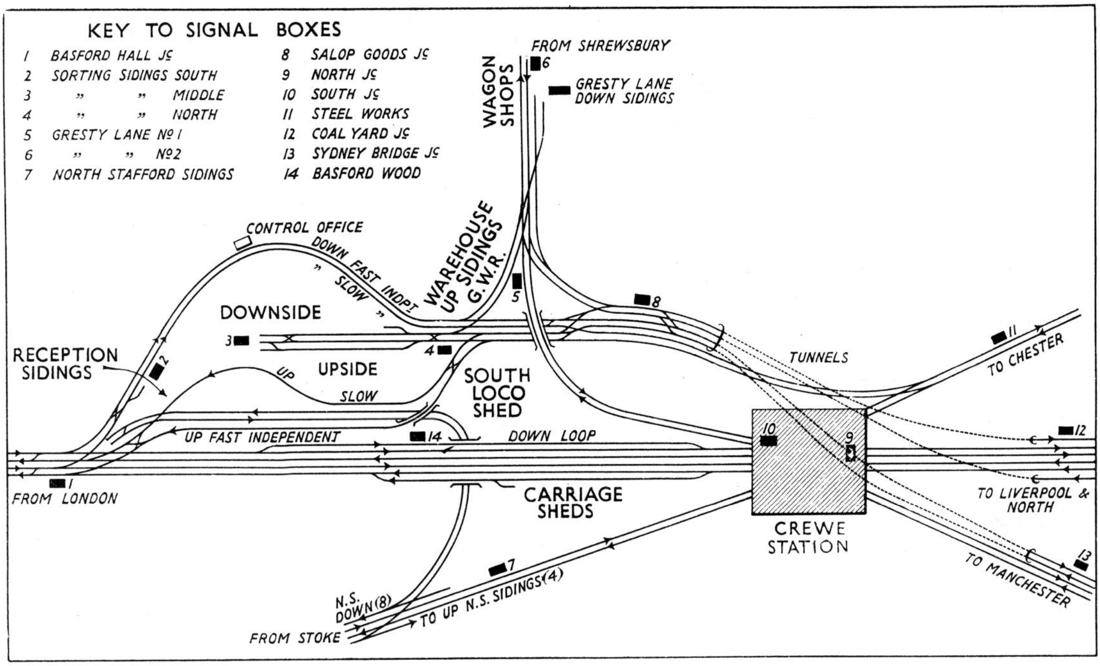

By courtesy of The Railway Magazine

Plan showing how the various lines approaching Crewe were interconnected and linked up with the sorting sidings.

Total staff	122,000
Locomotives	7,688
Rail motor vehicles	257
Coaching vehicles	23,422
Merchandise and mineral veh.	281,753
Service vehicles	14,343
No. of passenger trains daily	13,500
No. of freight trains daily	16,000
Engine miles per year	235,000,000
No. of passengers per year (approx)	460,000,000

Since the formation of the LMS much had been done to improve the utilisation of locomotives, involving a close co-operative effort between the departments of the Chief Operating Manager and the Chief Mechanical Engineer. On 1 January 1927 the total number of locomotives was 10,159, but by the end of 1937, as shown in the above table, this total had been reduced to 7,688, doing the same work. The engine miles per day had, indeed, been increased by 20 per cent. What was perhaps even more striking was that the mileage over which double-heading was required had been reduced by 37 per cent on passenger trains, and by no less than 61 per cent on freight. One would imagine that a major contributory factor to the latter improvement was due to the provision of much more powerful locomotives for the mineral trains of the Midland division, on which double-heading had previously been almost universal.

On the Western Division the freight train activities centred upon Crewe are largely obscured from an observer limited to 'spotting' from the platforms of the passenger station. At the turn of the century the LNWR completed a major scheme for expediting freight traffic by construction of the series of freight line tunnels at the north end of the station area, and the accompanying map shows in diagrammatic form the junctions, and their controlling signal-boxes in the 1930s. At that time in a normal week between 46,000 and 47,000 wagons, conveying all kinds of load and emanating from almost every corner of the British Isles were detached at Crewe. There were over 200 inward freight trains which detached, on an average, 7,000 wagons each 24 hours. After remarshalling those wagons were dispatched on 200 outward freight trains. A glance at the map will give some idea of the complexity of the movements involved. During periods of extreme pressure some non-stopping passenger trains were diverted via the freight tunnels, to relieve congestion in the station.

10
The Last Pre-War Year

In the King's Birthday Honours of 1938 Sir Josiah Stamp was raised to the peerage, and took the title Baron Stamp of Shortlands. He was proud of his association with the southern suburbs of London, and when the war came he always said he would not move from his big Victorian house until he was blown out of it – a challenge to the enemy that unhappily came only too true! But his honour, in 1938, could well have been taken as conferred on the LMS as a whole. No one of the four new companies had entered the grouping era encompassed by greater difficulties. That it had been developed into a strong, closely-knit and intensely progressive entity was in a very large measure due to Stamp's leadership, and his skill in getting the right men into the key position. At the same time one must not forget the part played by Sir Guy Granet in securing Stamp's services in the first place.

The summer of 1938 was, however, not otherwise a time for rejoicing. In Europe the international situation was becoming increasingly serious. The likelihood of war with Nazi Germany seemed to be growing more and more into an eventual certainty, and plans for the protection of vital parts of the railway organisation, such as traffic control centres, signal-boxes and such like against aerial attack were pressed forward. At the same time developments in the railway service were progressed with every outward impression of normality, notably in the complete re-casting of the express passenger train service of the Midland Division. In earlier schemes of acceleration preference had somewhat naturally been given to the former LNWR lines, as carrying by far the heavier traffic; but in 1938 the turn of the Midland had come, and this was in large measure a manifestation of the success and general reliability of the Stanier 5X class locomotives, after their rather shaky start. In 1938 no locomotives of the Royal Scot class were in regular service on the Midland. So far as fastest times went the accelerations could not be called spectacular, but so far as the complete service was concerned the improvements were substantial enough.

Reference to the lavish service to Manchester by the Midland route brings nostalgic memories, for to me it was much the pleasantest route from London. On my last pre-war journey, by the 2.30 pm from St Pancras, a 'Black Five' 4–6–0 with a load of no more than 255 tons was double-headed as far as Derby, but then, unaided, made short work of the mountain section, covering the 31½ miles to Millers Dale in 35½ minutes, where a stop was made to detach the through carriage for Buxton. We had time well in hand afterwards until a string of checks delayed the final approach to Manchester and made us 1½ minutes late on arrival.

In the late summer of 1938 everything was

MIDLAND DIVISION – JOURNEY TIMES FROM LONDON

City	Distance from St Pancras (miles)	Year	Fastest time (min.)	Complete Service No. of trains daily	Average time min.
LEICESTER	99	1914	106	22	110
		1936	106	22	112
		1937–8	99	23	104
MANCHESTER	190	1914	220	14	240
		1936	235	13	251
		1937–8	215	13	230
NOTTINGHAM	123½	1914	135	18	154
		1936	129	17	150
		1937–8	123	18	138
SHEFFIELD	158¼	1914	182	18	204
		1936	182	16	199
		1937–8	172	19	188

overshadowed by the rapidly worsening international situation, leading up to the crisis stemmed by the historic, if illusory Munich 'agreement' at the beginning of October. As the *Railway Gazette* commented editorially: 'The mere idea of the possibilities of aerial attack had crowded our main railway stations with "refugees" during the worst days. The ominous preparations, the gas masks, the trenches, the preparedness of the railways, even more than any military mobilisation, contributed to the anxiety of the people, with the effect that the nation was in direct contact with its Government to an extent which would have been impossible in previous emergencies, a fact which no doubt heartened the Premier in his great efforts. It is interesting to reflect that the advances of science which have brought the dread possibilities of war to our very doors, have also provided means of communication and transport without which a settlement might have been impossible.'

Whatever else may be said about the 'agreement' concluded by Neville Chamberlain at Munich it secured us a vital year in which to speed up preparations for what many, despite Munich, were convinced was inevitable.

In the midst of all the mounting anxiety the LMS did not falter in its plans to celebrate the opening throughout from London to Birmingham of what was the first main line inter-city railway anywhere in the world. The centenary of that great event came on 17 September 1938, and was marked by a notable exhibition at Euston, from the 19 to 25 September. Somewhat naturally, in view of the prevailing circumstances that exhibition was not visited by as many people as could have been wished; but for those who would delve into history the *Railway Gazette* published with its issue of 16 September a magnificent 84-page supplement, in which the whole subject of the centenary was treated comprehensively. It was good to see such locomotives as the 'Lion',

Author's Collection

55. The first taper-boilered 'Scot': no. 6170, 'British Legion', replacement for the ill-fated high-pressure compound 4–6–0 'Fury'.

'Coppernob' and 'Cornwall' at Euston, though a deep regret, retrospectively, is that the 'Coronation' of 1911 (George the Fifth class) so magnificently turned out in 1938, was not eventually preserved, as an example of the twentieth-century locomotive practice of Crewe Works. If restored to the LNWR livery, to accompany 'Hardwicke' she would have made a noble addition to the 'Rocket 150' cavalcade in May 1980.

Even though the international tension in Europe had been temporarily eased by the Munich agreement there were very serious matters for the LMS Board, as indeed there were for all the British railways. In the face of difficult freight traffic conditions the railways were seeking relief from the existing statutory regulation of the charges they could make for the conveyance of merchandise, realising how this situation put them at a serious disadvantage compared to road hauliers. The latter were well enough aware of what the railways had in mind, and even before the launching of the Square Deal campaign in November 1938 there had been a steadily increasing press campaign, conducted by the road haulage interests for the purpose of representing, or, as the *Railway Gazette* pungently expressed it, misrepresenting that the railway companies were trying to interfere with the right of the trader to select the form of transport which he approved, and which was more convenient to his purpose. Such, of course, was very far from the case. The railways did not seek preferential treatment. It was simply that they were being gravely injured by the one-sided control of their charges for the conveyance of merchandise, and that they were sure that serious national reactions would inevitably follow if they were denied the right to compete on equal terms with other forms of transport. It is a matter of history now that the Square Deal campaign, waged with much vigour in the press, and by huge banners and numerous posters at stations throughout the

Author's Collection

56. One of thirty diesel-electric 6-cylinder 350-hp shunting locomotives, with jackshaft drive, built at Derby in 1939, using English Electric engines.

country, did not get the sympathy it deserved, though early in 1939 events on the Continent of Europe began to push purely domestic affairs into the background.

In the dark days that followed the outbreak of war in September 1939 the strategic and tactical importance of railway marshalling yards was brought home forcibly to members of the general public by the treatment meted out to German yards by the RAF. The opening, therefore, of the large new mechanised yard at Toton, north of Trent, Midland Division, at the end of May, had a significance beyond even the prospect of greatly improved operation at that great concentration point for the coal traffic from the Nottinghamshire, Derbyshire, and South Yorkshire collieries. At that stage the modernisation was confined to the yard on the down side, which dealt with returning empties, sorting them for distribution to their owning collieries. Today it is perhaps not generally realised what an enormous burden the existence of vast quantities of privately owned wagons placed upon the railways. The operation at Toton Down Yard was fully mechanised, with power operated rail brakes, automatic setting of the more intensively used points, and a limited

57. Euston–Glasgow special for the Institution of Locomotive Engineers, June 1938, leaving Euston hauled by streamlined Pacific no. 6225, 'Duchess of Gloucester'.

BBC Hulton Picture Library

58. The down 'Mid-day Scot', passing Kilburn hauled by one of the non-streamlined Pacifics of the Duchess class in original condition, without smoke-deflector plates: no. 6231, 'Duchess of Atholl'.

Ian Allan Ltd

amount of colour light signalling in the approaches. Motive power for the hump shunting was entirely by diesel-electric locomotives. It was perhaps ironical that the railbrakes were of German design, of a type that had previously been used on the LNER at Whitemoor, and at Hull new inwards yard. Toton represented the latest practice in British fully mechanised yards, but it was not until after the war that other yards were equipped in a similar manner.

Another feature new to British practice, but prophetic of a major development after the war, was the interest being taken on the LMS in flat-bottomed rails. To some it seemed little short of sacrilege, particularly on a railway with such a large inheritance from the LNWR, that anything could be considered better than the traditional British bull head rail and chaired track. But without for one moment contemplating the slightest diminution in standards there were certain technical considerations that suggested an extended trial in main line service would be worthwhile. Apart from any other points, flat-bottomed rails have a greater lateral stiffness than bull headed rails of the same weight, and would thus be able to keep their 'line' with less maintenance. From the outset, of course, there was no question of spiking flat-bottomed rails directly to the sleepers, as on the majority of overseas railways. Specially designed cast iron bedplates were used in all the LMS trials, so shaped as to impart the standard degree of inward inclination to rails, as with bull head, to provide the centring effect characteristic of British track.

Much publicity and honour for the LMS was derived from the sending of a Coronation class streamlined Pacific locomotive and eight of the latest coaches to the New York World's Fair, as from 30 April 1939. The engine, which was finished in the streamlined style of 1937, but in standard maroon, instead of the royal blue of Coronation year, was actually no. 6229, 'Duchess of Hamilton', but numbered and named 6220, 'Coronation', for the tour. The train itself included a variety of stock not normally in the rake of the Coronation Scot train, with a first-class sleeping car, a club saloon car and a corridor first lounge. The show train was shipped from Southampton on 20 January 1939, and by a coincidence only a fortnight earlier I travelled to Liverpool behind

Author's Collection

59. Shipping the 'Coronation Scot' to the USA. Engine 6229, renumbered 6220 and named 'Coronation', at Southampton docks.

Author's Collection

60. The 'Coronation Scot' on exhibition at Chicago, alongside a New York Central 'Hudson' 4–6–4; Mr R. A. Riddles (right) is standing in front of the American locomotive.

the *real* 6220, then renumbered 6229 and renamed, but still in its original blue. I travelled behind the engine again, still in blue, in September 1940.

While I believe there was every intention to develop the lightweight high speed train precept further, from the initial experience in running the Coronation Scot in regular service between Euston and Glasgow, heavy load haulage remained the principal consideration with the Princess-Coronation class Pacific engines, and in February 1939 a test train of twenty vehicles, including the dynamometer car, was hauled without assistance at any point between Crewe and Glasgow and back again. As the tare load was no less than 604 tons, twice the weight of the Coronation Scot, and in wintry weather the conditions were far from favourable, especially on the mountain sections, this was a very severe test of locomotive capacity. The engine concerned was one of the non-streamlined members of the class, no. 6234, 'Duchess of Abercorn', significantly, perhaps, one that had a twin-orifice blastpipe and double chimney. The performance may be summarised thus:

Distance covered (train miles)	487.2
Net running time	516½ mins
Actual running time	532 mins 15 secs
Average speed mph	55.2 mph
Maximum speed mph	88 mph
Coal (excluding shed duties)	
lb. per mile	68.7
lb. per d.h.p. hour	3.12
lb. per square foot of grate area per hour (running time)	75.7
Water (excluding shed duties)	
Gallons per mile	53.1
lb. per d.h.p. hour	24.15
Evaporation lb. of water per lb. of coal	7.74

Considering that this round trip involved the unassisted ascents of the Shap and Beattock inclines, and the haulage of such a load as 604 tons the above were remarkable figures. In the northbound direction the minimum speeds on the two major inclines were 30 mph in each case.

The May timetables of 1939, which showed an aggregate daily mileage of 6,880 booked at speeds of 60 mph proved to be the climax of LMS train service development, because the onset of war four months later brought immediate and drastic deceleration, and there was no comparable recovery within the life of the Company. That brief period in the summer of 1939 also proved the swansong of the Royal Scot locomotives in their original form. As the third volume of this work will relate, they were subsequently rebuilt almost out of recognition. This volume may well be concluded by reference to one of the last runs I had with one of them, on the Aberdeen and Edinburgh section of the up 'Royal Scot' express, booked to cover the 299.2 miles from Carlisle to Euston, non-stop, in 299 minutes. The engine was no. 6132 then named 'The Kings Regiment (Liverpool)' and the load eleven coaches, 355 tons behind the tender. We covered the first 90.1 miles to Preston, almost exactly to time, in 94¾ minutes; but between there and Crewe a succession of delays caused a loss of 11 minutes, and the train was still 9½ minutes late on passing Stafford. But a clear road subsequently, and magnificent running, recovered the whole of the lost time in the 100.2 miles thence to Tring – 84¼ minutes actual, instead of the 94 minutes scheduled; and the train ran 'on time' thence to the arrival in Euston. It was a pleasant memory to carry into the days of crowded, decelerated, and much delayed trains of the war years.

Index